# TIFFANY
# TABLE SETTINGS

# TIFFANY
# TABLE SETTINGS

BRAMHALL HOUSE · NEW YORK

This edition published by Bramhall House,
a division of Clarkson N. Potter,
by arrangement with Thomas Y. Crowell Company

c  d  e  f  g  h

# PREFACE

In 1956 Tiffany & Co., the famous Fifth Avenue jewelers and silversmiths, inaugurated an active program to present table settings of taste and imagination to the public. The purpose of this program—a continual round of exhibitions—is to inspire and provoke greater interest in this area of design. When the exhibits are held, thousands of people visit Tiffany's weekly to view the settings by New York's leading hostesses and interior decorators. The store holds that a "perfect party" implies a beautiful table as well as a distinguished menu. Those who are chosen to design tables select Tiffany china, silver, and glass as accessories on their tables, combining these elements with their own furniture, linens, and antiques.

This collection of settings has not been compiled to instruct in the "book of etiquette" sense. Rather, it is hoped that the presentation of these settings will be a source of inspiration and a focus of ideas to any hostess.

There is infinite variety of design in these tables. Some of the settings are based on the theory of switching objects created for one purpose to other uses, as well as juggling to make new combinations of color, fabric, and shape. Some of the settings are classic examples of subtle orthodox statement. Others are frankly based on fantasy.

The common denominator of good style, however, underlies all the designs, regardless of the occasion or spirit of formality or informality. A table set with inexpensive earthenware, for example, on a checked cotton cloth can be as enticing and appetizing as one of rare porcelain, crystal, and silver.

The editors believe that a woman is not using her own creative abilities unless she can turn her imagination to lending a fresh look to her table. It is hoped that this book will encourage a new point of view in this field of interior design.

# CONTENTS

# TIFFANY
# TABLE SETTINGS

# THE ANTIQUE CENTERPIECE

The antique centerpiece has always been a handsome focal point for table settings. In this section a variety of tables show how countless decorative moods can be achieved by using a beautiful bowl, épergne, crystal or porcelain object of another era to grace the center of the table. Whether the container is enhanced by an arrangement of fruit, flowers, and leaves, or left empty to highlight its form, such a centerpiece can dominate any table with authority—including settings of an otherwise informal flavor.

## Dinner Around a Crystal Temple

MRS. WILLIAM WOODWARD *Tiffany Hostesses' Show*

Mrs. William Woodward uses as a centerpiece for her table her tall, unusual Waterford crystal "perfume temple," which was formerly use to burn perfumed oil during the dinner party. This time she has filled the center with a group of persimmons, to provide a strong color accent. The color of the fruit is picked up in the china pattern of rich Imari colors (cobalt blue, tangerine, and gold). She uses her antique Waterford crystal girandoles on either side of the temple, and antique crystal salts and peppers. The oval mats are of delicate old rosepoint lace, with napkins of heavy white linen embroidered with the family crest. Elaborate sterling flatware and crystal patterns are Mrs. Woodward's choices to complete the setting.

# A Dinner with Antique Silver

MRS. CHARLES SUYDAM CUTTING *Tiffany Hostesses' Show*

Mrs. Charles Suydam Cutting has set a table that is a jewel of antique silver. She has used her own table ornaments: cigarette boxes for each place with hunting scenes sculptured in low relief; an Irish potato ring for the center of the table; columnar Irish candlesticks; cups, bowls, and all sorts of objects from the Charles II, Queen Anne, and early Georgian periods. She has made an unusual arrangement of pomegranates and grapes, red ampelopsis, and brown cyprepedium from her greenhouses for the center decoration. Mrs. Cutting's écru fine linen cloth is embroidered with "Dixiana," the name of her plantation. The finely monogrammed napkins are from France. She uses a simple English reproduction sterling flatware pattern, and a very plain stemware pattern. The dinner plates are white, with a subtle gold scratch-line decoration on the scalloped border.

Mrs. Cutting has grouped her antique silver objects on the table for decorative as well as for utilitarian purposes. The warm tone of the cream-colored cloth brings forth the glow of the old silver.

4

# Dinner Designed to Emphasize the China Pattern

MRS. MELLON BRUCE *Tiffany Hostesses' Show*

Mrs. Mellon Bruce has created here a traditional table for six, designed to dramatize and highlight her rare antique Coalport china. The result is a harmony of color and design. The gold and yellow dinner plates are placed on écru lace mats. To maintain the golden look, Mrs. Bruce uses vermeil flatware. The crystal is swag-patterned, and the centerpiece is an elaborate compotière, left empty and guarded with four crystal candlesticks. Other matching pieces on the table are a pair of oyster dishes and a pair of covered sauce tureens. Footed salts and peppers, ashtrays, and assorted boxes in a woven basket texture, all in vermeil, complete the setting.

## The Monumental Centerpiece

MR. ROBERT SAMUELS OF FRENCH & CO.
*Tiffany Decorators' Show*

French & Co. has designed this dinner setting, using their own furnishings. The long oval reproduction Louis XVI table features a white marbleized top on an elaborately carved gilt base. The Louis XVI chairs, again of gilt wood, are covered in a rich ivory silk and trimmed in gold piping. The setting is placed on a nineteenth-century Savonnerie rug of warm browns, beiges, and rose tints. An extraordinary centerpiece is the long mirrored plateau with bronze doré dancing nymphs in a group at each end, designed by Pierre Thomire in the nineteenth century. The gallery of the plateau is heavily ornamented with classic figures and candle holders, and the nymph groups bear aloft épergnes with a relief of grape clusters. The floral arrangement combines white orchids with grapes and apples, and in the center of the plateau is a tree of gold-sprayed leaves interspersed with white roses.

Elaborate gold-encrusted white china is used on white embroidered place mats. Vermeil flatware and accessories, and goblets with air-twist stems complete this rich gold and white setting.

Mrs. Kellogg sets a table with her rare, écru-colored crèpe de chine tablecloth and matching napkins. In the center of the cloth ancient lace depicts scenes from the Crusades. For the center of the table she uses one of her tall, imposing Waterford crystal candelabra on a marble base, with two graceful swags of crystal rising to a center pinnacle. Mrs. Kellogg has selected orange and gold Lowestoft reproduction plates of the armorial type (a repetition of the swag design), combined with a vermeil flatware pattern and accessories. The square bases of the goblets repeat that of the Waterford centerpiece. Her table has a look of simplicity in color and in objects, so as to place the emphasis on the centerpiece and linens.

MRS. FRANCIS L. KELLOGG
*Tiffany Hostesses' Show*

# Dinner Party with a Waterford Candelabra

## "La Favorita"

VALERIAN RYBAR, INC. *Tiffany Decorators' Show*

Valerian Rybar has decorated a sumptuous eighteenth-century table, inspired by "La Favorita," the famous Palazzino Cinese in Palermo, Sicily, which was the residence in exile of Ferdinando IV of Naples. Eighteenth-century Italian gilt armchairs upholstered in apple-green taffeta are drawn up to an oval mahogany table. The embroidered place mats and napkins are of crushed-strawberry-color organdy, cut in a baroque shape. Hand-painted plates with chinoiserie figures on the border, vermeil flatware with a similar decorative motif, and all vermeil accessories are used. These harmonize with the elaborate centerpiece, a cut crystal and ormolu chinoiserie temple, holding a rare eighteenth-century Meissen chinoiserie porcelain figurine. The pavilion is decorated with miniature fruits and flowers by Mr. Rybar, as are the gilt obelisks and Louis XV bronze doré candlesticks surrounding it. The table and chairs are placed on a large antique Bessarabian rug in soft green and rose colors which repeat the color scheme of the table.

# The Antique Vegetable Luncheon

MRS. GILBERT MILLER *Tiffany Hostesses' Show*

Mrs. Gilbert Miller has designed a luncheon setting in a harmonious color scheme of fresh green and golden beige, to display her exquisite antique porcelain vegetables. These Chelsea and Chinese *objets d'art* would enhance any kind of setting. The round shapes of the green-fern-decorated plates are repeated in the écru linen and lace place mats. The embroidery of these mats seems to repeat even the design motifs of the china. Very plain stemware and sterling flatware blend into the two-color scheme. Even the white wine in the decanter becomes an important color accent here.

# The Silver Tureen Dinner

MRS. LYTLE HULL *Tiffany Hostesses' Show*

Mrs. Lytle Hull has set a formal dinner for eight, built around a fascinating collection of French nineteenth-century covered tureens, with finials in the shape of various vegetables.

A feeling of height is achieved by the use of four stately columnar silver candlesticks and goblets with air twist stems. Mrs. Hull places rose-colored, eighteenth-century reproduction armorial soft paste plates on white organdy mats, and her antique porcelain cigarette cups and sterling ashtrays add the finishing touches to the simple table which she has designed to show the unusual tureens to their best advantage.

# A Favrile Collector Entertains

VAN DAY TRUEX *Tiffany Decorators' Show*

Van Truex has used Tiffany glass in a delightful "art nouveau" setting. But he has also translated these late nineteenth-century elements into a contemporary setting. A circular cloth of heavy natural linen with white embroidered flowers covers the round table. The rug is a warm beige needlepoint with a border of pastel flowers. English Regency black lacquered chairs with cane seats are drawn up to the table.

On the table Mr. Truex uses a variety of glass bowls and stemware, each one showing the delicate coloring of Louis Comfort Tiffany's invention, as well as his genius for designing fluid, balanced shapes. A bowl full of kumquats soars on a tall graceful stem in the center, surrounded by two different pairs of glass candlesticks, which, with their long white tapers, lend a Gothic feeling. Florid gold and white bone china plates are used, as well as vermeil flatware and small vermeil accessories. Everything else on the table, from the tiny nut dishes to the goblets and flowerlike finger bowls, is in Louis C. Tiffany's favrile glass. Mr. Truex's use of kumquats, tangerines, lemon gumdrops, and chocolates wrapped in "art nouveau" paper, in conjunction with the multicolored favrile glass, achieves the effect of bathing the whole setting in a beige glow with yellow, orange, violet, and blue rainbow tints. One orchid, casually placed, serves as an accent.

# A Dinner in Pink Around a Sweetmeat Tree

MRS. NATHANIEL BOWDITCH POTTER *Tiffany Hostesses' Show*

Mrs. Potter's dinner party for four is a confection of pink and white crystal. On a round antique table, she uses a pale pink damask cloth with matching napkins bearing the family crest in white embroidery. In the center of the table is a tall antique crystal "sweetmeat dish," holding pink and white candies and flowers in its separate cups. She surrounds it with her tall and short Waterford crystal candlesticks, pink opaline butter plates, and pink Bristol ashtrays. From Tiffany Mrs. Potter has used china in a rose bird design, in conjunction with a palm-motif flatware. She also selects a crystal pattern to match the Waterford crystal in feeling. Louis XV chairs with rose leather seats complete a delightful *"vie en rose"* mood for this decorative dinner party.

MRS. JOHN R. DREXEL III

*Tiffany Hostesses' Show*

Mrs. John R. Drexel III sets a luncheon table for four to high-light her centerpiece—an eighteenth-century English cut-crystal and silver-gilt épergne. She has filled it with a variety of fruits in green and rose colors and combined with it green and white plates on round white linen place mats appliquéd with coral flowers.

Mrs. Drexel chooses shell-handled flatware in vermeil and a crystal pattern which matches the épergne cutting. With the dessert, cheese, and fruit Mrs. Drexel serves red wine from a crystal and vermeil decanter. As table ornaments she uses three vermeil boxes in the forms of a shiny artichoke, a lemon, and an orange.

There is an attractive contrast of the almost "country look" kind of informality in the china pattern, linens, and vegetable boxes with the formality of the cut crystal centerpiece and vermeil flatware.

# A Luncheon Around a Crystal and Vermeil Épergne

Mrs. John Pierrepont sets a formal dinner for twelve on an unusual eighteenth-century English Hepplewhite table made of San Domingo mahogany. She uses place mats no larger than the dinner plates to show off the beautiful sheen of the wood. With the lace mats she uses heavy monogrammed damask napkins.

The accent, however, is on Mrs. Pierrepont's impressive centerpiece, filled with boxwood and flowers. The early nineteenth-century dancing figures are of gold and white Capo di Monte porcelain.

Mrs. Pierrepont chooses a white French china with a gold border encrusted with roses, and a classic crystal pattern. Red and white wine are placed at either end of the table in large clear crystal decanters. She uses sterling flatware, but her dessert flatware is in vermeil, placed at the head of the dinner plates according to European custom. The menus are held by vermeil pineapple holders.

# The Capo Di Monte Table

MRS. JOHN PIERREPONT
*Tiffany Hostesses' Show*

17

# Dinner for Ten Around a Silver Temple

MRS. J. GORDON DOUGLAS
*Tiffany Hostesses' Show*

Mrs. J. Gordon Douglas plans her elegant table for ten around her collection of eighteenth-century silver table ornaments. Her hand-crafted French centerpiece with fluted columns—called "The Temple of Love"—is flanked by two pairs of Corinthian-column Georgian candlesticks, very much in the same feeling as the center structure. Put to modern use are other antique pieces: a pair of Irish pierced potato rings, used here to hold grapes, and a pair of sterling wine-tasters, doubling as ashtrays.

Mrs. Douglas chooses a flatware pattern which has the same border —a popular motif of the eighteenth century—as her own period salts and peppers. She uses an elegant gold and rose china pattern and heavy crystal goblets with a Gothic cutting.

Showing a preference for the bare table look, Mrs. Douglas has limited her linens to elaborately monogrammed heavy beige linen napkins. As an added touch, a pale green orchid floats in the silver temple.

# WORKS OF ART
# ON THE TABLE

Art has its place on a table, too, as is illustrated in these settings which include everything from silver and marble sculptures to antique and contemporary figurines and paintings. There are many ways to integrate works of art gracefully into the centerpiece decorations, for art treasures taken from their usual display area and placed in a new setting assume a fresh dimension and interest.

The following settings all have one common factor: the use of flowers to lend softness and decorative accent to the objects dominating the table.

## A Luncheon with a Sculpture Centerpiece

MRS. DAN P. CAULKINS
*Tiffany Hostesses' Show*

Mrs. Dan P. Caulkins uses a cornflower blue and white color scheme in her springlike luncheon setting on a round table. Her centerpiece is a white marble rabbit on an ebony base, sculpted by her sister, Jane Canfield. The rabbit seems to be sitting in a field of flowers— an effect achieved by four cut-crystal crescents filled with blue and white flowers on a mirrored plateau. Her tablecloth is blue linen with snow-white fringe. With it she uses blue-flowered china with touches of gold. The porcelain flatware in gold and white matches the china in feeling, and delicate-stemmed crystal reflects the blue of the cloth.

Mrs. Caulkins places her table on a blue and white Spanish rug (not visible in the photograph) of the exact same shade as the tablecloth and uses Regency chairs. The rug is an important part of the overall scheme.

# The Silver Knights

MRS. BYRNES MACDONALD *Tiffany Hostesses' Show*

On a bare mahogany surface, Mrs. Byrnes MacDonald sets a blue and silver table with an antique emphasis. She places antique silver figurines in the center of the setting. A tall pyramid floral arrangement of blue and white flowers is built on a base of a gay assortment of oranges, grapes, and cherries. Guarding the flowers in the center are Mrs. MacDonald's two pairs of dashing knights in full armor, made of sterling silver in eighteenth-century Germany. Two of the knights are on horseback, charging with lances, and two are standing figures. Visored caps lift to reveal chivalrous ivory faces beneath.

The blue of the cornflowers is repeated in the blue and gray stoneware pattern. Mrs. MacDonald uses antique silver candelabra, salts and peppers, and a reproduction flatware pattern, including pistol-handled knives, which has an early English feeling. A crystal pattern with a marked swag motif repeats the swag of the plate design.

MRS. ALBERT D. LASKER
*Tiffany Hostesses' Show*

Mrs. Albert D. Lasker has set a luncheon table for eight, all in white except for the bright accent of anemones, which, mixed with white carnations, ring the white figurines. These antique Blanc de Chine pieces depicting goddesses seem to be rising from seas of flowers —an effect achieved by planting them in curved crystal rings.

Mrs. Lasker uses white bone china with a wavy fluted edge on delicate white organdy mats with a similar wavy pattern. Simple crystal goblets and sterling flatware finish the graceful setting.

# The White Luncheon

This setting, designed to show off the group of "Oriental Musician" sculptures by Andrea Spadini, has an eighteenth-century air of elegance that is also contemporary. The plates with a plum-colored pattern are displayed on a pale green brocade cloth. Flatware and accessories—shell ashtrays, fish-shaped salts and peppers, artichoke boxes—are all in vermeil. Elaborately cut crystal is an added note of formality.

In the center, the six white Spadini ceramic figurines surround a central urn filled with multicolored violets. Some of the smaller white urn-cups are used to hold cigarettes; others serve as candle holders. The musicians are rendered in animated movement, each playing an oriental instrument and dressed in an elaborate costume with turban.

*The*

*Oriental*

*Musicians*

# THE SPADINI GROUPS

In the spring of 1960 Tiffany introduced a new concept in table decorations—the Spadini groups. Andrea Spadini, a famous Roman sculptor, was commissioned by the store to make ten different groups of ceramic sculptured figures—each set unique, one of a kind, and made without molds so that no more would ever be made. The sculptor succeeded in translating into the medium of ceramics his gift for sculpture that is Baroque and yet twentieth-century, full of movement but contained, monumental but precious in a small size, dignified but permeated with a sense of humor.

The public seized upon this idea of grouped figures with enthusiasm. It is felt that the Spadini influence on American table decorations and centerpiece themes will have an ever-increasing importance.

When not in use on the table as a centerpiece group, the Spadini figurines fit with equal ease into any part of the decor of the home—on a table, a library shelf, a mantelpiece, in a wall niche. As works of art, they were designed primarily for the table. As gay sculptures full of verve and vitality, they are a delight to the eye anywhere.

A circus of Spadini ceramic figurines, each one representing a different set of six or more figures, to decorate formal or informal table settings. From the left, an elephant balancing a pink ball, a rhinoceros balancing a blue ball, two dancing bears, a prancing pony, and a monkey modeling a leafy hat while admiring himself in a mirror.

## Spadini Elephants

A delightful group of the Spadini figurines for table settings—the "Frolicking Elephants." The white ceramic pachyderms, trimmed in pink, are shown capering about on their pedestals, balancing and juggling pink balls. Six individual flower urns and a round center bowl are filled with flowers and greenery.

This group was set on a table with pink and white china, and with pink and white linens.

Happily gamboling rhinoceroses make up one of the Spadini groups. In white ceramic, touched with accents of blue, the animals are gaily playing on their pedestals around a rather matronly rhinoceros who seems to be urging them to behave. The central figure, with a bowl on its back for flower arrangements, has all of the dignity of the elephant obelisk in the center of one of Rome's most famous piazzas.

# Spadini
# Rhinoceroses

# Epicures and Connoisseurs

RAYMOND LOEWY *Tiffany Decorators' Show*

Mr. Loewy designs a dinner for three among modern and antique art treasures. His theme is that one should live in an integral relationship with one's art collection in the home, and not just admire it from afar.

Dinner is set on a teakwood table. The terra-cotta red chairs are Italian Directoire with beige silk seats. A large rug (not visible in the photograph) was specially designed by Mr. Loewy for this exhibit; it features a large rose raised on a soft beige ground.

The dinner service, everything from large service plates to napkin rings, is all in vermeil. Heavy cylindrical crystal tumblers are used for water and wine. Three white camellias float in a crystal bowl in the center, accompanied by one large white candle set on a vermeil dish. Pale green, beige, and black napkins accent the setting, as does the white conch bowl filled with greens. The dinner setting is at one end of the table. Objects from the host's art collection are highlighted at the other end: a Picasso still-life painted in 1914, and an Egyptian stone fragment from King Amen Hotep's reign in 1600 B.C. A Strobic plastic mobile construction hangs above the table. Everything is spotlighted to bring out detail. Behind these objects is a wall tapestry of an eighteenth-century Gobelin design, depicting "The Breakfast of the Sultana." The marriage of past and present is further enhanced by the play of light thrown across the antique tapestry by the movement of the spotlighted mobile. Even a round crystal clock finds its place on this unusual table, a subtle reminder to busy executives or punctual theatergoers.

*The word "informal" does not imply a hastily thrown together table. The art of creating the informal table is as exacting and difficult as planning a formal dinner party. The following tables, which for the most part look deceptively simple, show a careful study of color and other elements.*

# THE INFORMAL TABLE

William Pahlmann Associates have designed a luncheon setting in a decorator's studio, in essence, a working lunch for decorator and client. An unusual table, the top mounted on an antique painted Spanish base, is set on a tigerskin rug. The floor is polished Versailles parquet. The two Spanish side chairs are completely covered in a soft sea-green fabric printed with gold.

A four-panel French provincial walnut screen flanked by tree-plants provides the backdrop for the setting; each panel is beautifully carved with Renaissance motifs. A brass umbrella stand beside the table is filled to overflowing with fabric swatches and blueprints. An apothecary's wood chest, painted green-gold, is placed on the table, its drawers open to reveal pencils, color charts, and material samples. More swatches lie on the table, together with other tools of the designer's trade—ruler, blueprint, measuring tape, and drawings. A green basket full of marigolds and the bright orange linen napkins add touches of strong color to the table. The plates feature hand-painted designs of musical instruments on a toast-colored knotty wood background. Tall goblets cut in a Gothic arch pattern are combined with a simple sterling flatware pattern and sterling salts and pepper mills.

Additional accent is provided by a luxurious little cigarette box by Schlumberger of Tiffany (black pinseal lined with 18-karat gold), a green leaf-shaped ashtray, and a porcelain box in the shape of a large walnut.

*Designer-Client Luncheon*

WILLIAM PAHLMANN ASSOCIATES, INC.
*Tiffany Decorators' Show*

31

# The Vegetable Luncheon

MRS. HAROLD E. TALBOTT *Tiffany Hostesses' Show*

Mrs. Harold E. Talbott's "vegetable party" is a riot of color, beginning with her tablecloth and matching napkins embroidered in bright designs of all types of vegetables. In the center is a veritable family of cabbages; a large green eighteenth-century French one is surrounded by four smaller English and Portuguese ones. All of these *objets d'art* have removable lids, and they are part of Mrs. Talbott's unique collection of antique vegetables displayed in the dining room of her home.

The china is a stark white design, wrought in a cabbage motif. Simple, unpatterned shapes in accessories, including the large sterling salt and pepper grinder sets, ashtrays in porringer shapes, and white porcelain-handled flatware, complete the setting.

McMillen Inc. has designed this luncheon in a combination of traditional and contemporary elements. The hostess is a collector of modern art, and the dominating factor of the dining scene is a large abstract oil in soft yellows, blues, and white. The yellow and blue of the painting are picked up again in the rug and chairs. The Louis XVI reproduction chairs are covered in a Far Eastern silk of striped yellow, dark green, and light green. The rug, designed in rectangles of blue and green by George Nelson, is a strong contemporary accent.

The table is French, a dark green lacquer top on a contemporary base, designed by Gilbert Poillerat. White organdy mats and napkins are used, and the white accent is repeated in the blue and white flowers filling the crystal sweetmeat tree (reproduction, nineteenth-century) in the center of the table. Four small crystal vases guarding the tree are filled with primroses. White bone china with a touch of gold on its border is used with matching bone china and vermeil flatware. Crystal soups, butter plates, and very simple stemware complete this uncluttered table setting.

The effect is a happy combination of the eighteenth, nineteenth, and twentieth centuries, done in accents of yellow, blue, and green.

# *Luncheon in Green, Blue, and Yellow*

MCMILLEN INC.
*Tiffany Decorators' Show*

# A Study in Gray, Gold, and White

MRS. VINCENT ASTOR *Tiffany Hostesses' Show*

Mrs. Vincent Astor's table is done in gray and gold in a disarmingly effortless manner. The gray scene-decorated centerpiece bowl with gold rim is left empty to permit full view of its decoration; and a ring of white lilacs surrounds the bowl, intersected by four vermeil cups holding white roses.

Gray leaves and grapes form the border decoration for the plates. Vermeil flatware, candlesticks, and holloware carry forth the gold accent of the table. The accessories are very simple in shape; the embroidered white organdy linens repeat the leaf theme in their design.

## A Salad Centerpiece Luncheon

A vitamin-charged setting designed to raise wilting spirits during a heat wave is set on a cloth of heavy white linen embroidered with vegetables. The solid-colored napkins pick up the vegetable colors.

A well-chilled salad of vegetables fills the light mahogany and silver salad bowl; sterling-handled salad servers lie nearby. In spite of the classic notes of a simple sterling flatware pattern, sterling salts and peppers, and crystal cruets for salad dressing, the whole mood of the table is one of light-hearted informality.

The hand-painted ceramic plates depict different fruits. The hobnail iced-tea glasses can also be used for beer glasses or as water tumblers. Straw baskets filled with fruit and flowers "à l'Italienne," and cigarette urns and ashtrays dotted with ladybugs, reinforce the rustic theme.

William Baldwin's luncheon has an undeniable look of spring warmth, regardless of the weather outside. Bathed in yellows, blues, and greens, there is design interest in the floral centerpiece, the china, and the seat pads—three distinctly separate patterns that maintain an integral relationship with one another.

On a bare round surface Mr. Baldwin uses plates with a design of blue cornflowers on white. Cornflowers appear again in the white urn centerpiece, with the added freshness of daisies and greenery. Yellow is repeated in the golden vermeil flatware and table accessories. White wine is served in green tinted Rhine wine glasses.

Of major importance in the decorative scheme are the Regency chairs with seat pads covered in a white cotton fabric splashed with tiny blue flowers and big yellow butterflies.

# Luncheon for Four in a White Room

BALDWIN & MARTIN INC.
*Tiffany Decorators' Show*

# *Time Out*

MRS. HENRY PARISH II, INC. *Tiffany Decorators' Show*

Mrs. Henry Parish II has designed a charming luncheon setting for mother and infant daughter—a pause in the midst of the mother's work on her correspondence. A round table becomes a desk, covered to the floor with a circular cloth of cotton printed with brilliant red, purple, and blue flowers. A writing folder, red feather quill pen, antique Napoleonic bronze inkstand, antique English porcelain box, ivory seal, and basket of crest-engraved notepaper lie on the table. The flower motif is seen in the embroidered white organdy linens on the square luncheon tray and in the eighteenth-century English Battersea taper sticks. Large sunflowers in a French earthenware vase dominate the setting. The luncheon tray is set for the fruit or salad course; a hand-painted apple is the central motif on each plate. All accessories, including the flatware, owl-shaped jar, salt and pepper with pheasant finials, and peanut-shaped pillbox, are vermeil. An antique highchair is drawn up next to the mother's chair; baby has her own golden vermeil mug, porringer, pusher, and spoon. A six-panel French screen, an unusual eighteenth-century piece with painted fruit motifs, provides the backdrop as well as strong additional pattern interest.

A final delightful touch is a snapshot of the decorator's own daughter and grandchild on the table.

# The Tea-Kettle Table

Spring fever has struck this table with a charming vengeance. A cozy teakettle stuffed to its spout with spring flowers becomes a centerpiece of great dash. A little courage is required. But really only a little imagination is needed to enliven the table, amuse and delight the guests, and provide a never-ending conversation piece. The hostess can alternate the centerpiece container as often as she alters her menus and guest lists.

The theme of this table is blue and white, with scene-decorated earthenware; a simple silver pattern; heavy, handsomely cut goblets; and small white bisque urns holding white flowers at each place. The cloth is white linen with a design of blue leaves.

MCMILLEN INC. *Tiffany Decorators' Show*

## *Breakfast for Two*

McMillen Inc. has designed a setting for two people who like to have breakfast together but still like to maintain a degree of independence at that early hour. An S-curved loveseat in a gay yellow, lavender, and white fabric sets the color scheme. In front of each seat a small table is drawn up, one with a yellow and white embroidered organdy cloth, and the other with a mauve and white organdy cloth. Two different English bone china breakfast sets are used—one in a colored polka dot design, the other with fresh green and blue flowers on white. A little flower arrangement in a silver sugar bowl and another in a crystal bud vase add sparkle to the tables. A separate modernistic marble table on a spiral bronze base, also in a contemporary feeling, holds the sterling coffee and chocolate pots.

## *Breakfast at Tiffany's*    MRS. WILLIAM S. PALEY *Tiffany Hostesses' Show*

Although Mrs. Paley named her setting in honor of Truman Capote's novel of the same name, the inspiration is obviously directed toward creating a cozy repast for two people, complete with time for conversation and reading. Mrs. Paley's couple sit down to breakfast in their favorite chairs—his, an antique Louis XV leather wingback; hers, a French country chair in a green and white striped

fabric with matching ottoman. The same fresh green and white
striped fabric is used on the white wooden screen. Even the wooden
lamp with the white shade sports a green stripe.

There is pattern and color interest everywhere. A riot of green
flowers covers the circular cloth which falls to the floor; over this
Mrs. Paley places fine white linen mats and napkins. She uses a green
thistle-on-white pattern of English bone china. The result of a combination of formal with rustic, of contemporary with antique, is
a fascinating mélange of objects on the table: the antique English
silver flatware and coffee set; the straw basket for brioches; the black
basalt porcupine, with fresh green mignonette filling the holes on its
back; the silver chafing dish; heavy crystal tumblers, the antique
porcelain boxes and the green Bristol glass ashtrays.

# *Family Sunday Breakfast*

Sunday is the one day when the whole family can breakfast together in leisurely fashion. A prettily set table, such as this one in fresh blue and white, will be a welcome beginning to the day. The white linen napkins on an electric blue cotton cloth, the earthenware with its lively floral pattern in blue on white, and the white cabbage-leaf bowl in the center piled high with fresh fruit provide an appetizing background for the day's first meal. The orange juice served in a wine decanter and a silver turtle box provide conversation pieces, and even boiled eggs take on a new look when served in a matching earthenware soup tureen.

The crystal is simple and sturdy, from the two-part serving bowl for jam and honey and the coupe-shaped butter dish to the old-fashioned glasses and highball glasses, which are used here for water and orange juice. White porcelain-handled flatware adds yet another note of charm. In spite of its formal design, the Jack Sheppard-style sterling silver coffee set looks right at home on this table.

# *Breakfast in Bed*

MCMILLEN INC. *Tiffany Decorators' Show*

"Breakfast in bed" inspired McMillen to do a predominently white setting. The Italian rococo bed is white, accented with mint green, rising to a tall rectangular canopy with wide curtains of white pine-apple cloth. A white crèpe de chine and satin coverlet combines with white linen sheets heavily enbroidered in lace. This luxurious bed, thought to have come from one of the Palladian villas near Venice, appropriately rests on a white fur rug.

Breakfast served by such a bed must obviously be served in the grand manner. A contemporary round marble table on a bronze base is drawn up to hold the coffee service. The pattern of the china breakfast service is one of blue and green flowers on white. Pink sweetheart roses in a graceful water goblet add the final touch of freshness.

To the fortunate one being served breakfast in bed, here is a tray with little touches to bring added pleasure to the meal. The English bone china breakfast set is an intricate pattern of pink and blue flowers on white. The silver and crystal, in contrast, are simple and undecorated. A tiny salt and pepper set, designed especially for a breakfast tray, is used along with a silver pear box filled with honey. The saccharine bowl, with rose finial, has its own miniature tongs. The contemporary crystal has been borrowed from the bar: a highball glass doubles as a vase for fresh daisies, and the matching martini glass is filled with apple juice. And a final surprise—the morning newspapers, all tied with satin ribbon, look like an unexpected gift.

# *The Breakfast Tray*

# THE COUNTRY LOOK

Mrs. J. Lightfoot Walker sets a gay country luncheon table for four. Vegetables, fruit, flowers, and turtles grace the table in easy harmony. Mrs. Walker has used her eighteenth-century Brussels faïence cabbage as the centerpiece, and her tablecloth is embroidered with ears of corn. The faïence plates are hand-painted with cabbage roses; the eighteenth-century pistol-handled white porcelain flatware is also in keeping with the china.

Mrs. Walker introduces a new idea for wine lovers: a pair of small crystal decanters, one containing red wine, the other white, is placed in front of each place setting—the wine to be poured to taste into oversized glasses.

Silver turtles (actually boxes) creep out from under the cabbage, under the watchful eyes of the snails attached to the leaves. Silver apple and pear boxes, casually placed, reinforce the country look.

*Country*

*Luncheon*

*au Nature*

MRS. J. LIGHTFOOT WALKER
*Tiffany Hostesses' Show*

# Dinner for Three

MRS. LEWIS A. LAPHAM *Tiffany Hostesses' Show*

Using her favorite color combination of green and blue, Mrs. Lewis Lapham has done a setting for three. The table is a contemporary round wormy chestnut pedestal type, placed on a round emerald-green rug. The black and gold chairs are English Regency, and the blue-green Siamese silk chair seats, tied on with green silk tassels, are an important decorative accent. A cabbage rose design graces the scalloped borders of the quilted blue silk mats; the silk napkins are pale blue.

Mrs. Lapham has filled her centerpiece bowl of antique black basalt with pachysandra grown on her New Canaan place. With her dinner bell—a converted school bell, bronze on a malachite base—and green malachite cigarette box, she uses all vermeil accessories, including the shell-handled flatware, and an elaborately cut crystal pattern. The stoneware plates are decorated in warm blue with gold rims, in keeping with the color scheme.

# Sunday Luncheon on the Eleventh Floor

MRS. ALISON BISGOOD
*"Fashions in Living" Editor,*
VOGUE *Magazine*

Mrs. Alison Bisgood captures the luminous quality of a Vermeer painting in a rustic luncheon set in a corner of her Manhattan apartment. The scene seems to be bathed in a diffused light.

Mrs. Bisgood uses a clear blue and white scene-printed earthenware, delicate-stemmed goblets for the wine, old English reproduction sterling silver flatware, sterling shell ashtrays, salts and peppers in egg shapes, and vermeil menu holders. Her polished mother-of-pearl seashell centerpiece dish is filled with fruit and shells.

The circular tablecloth of green and white checked silk falls to the floor in graceful folds and is covered with an embroidered white linen tea cloth. The green and white of the cloth is echoed by the pale green grapes of the centerpiece, Mrs. Bisgood's jade cigarette urns, and the leaves of the Flemish type of still-life flower arrangement. Although the flowers are not the centerpiece decoration, they are an integral part of the structure of the setting, as are the antique country chairs with their heavy green fabric seat pads.

In using the compact space of her apartment, Mrs. Bisgood transforms the ledge of the window into a sideboard for most of the serving dishes. A small trifoliated table holds a sterling silver chafing dish and her faïence asparagus stalk sauce dish.

# The Barnyard Look

A luncheon setting in an utterly countrified style, to delight the eye and to amuse the spectator, is shown here. A sense of humor is the essential factor in the atmosphere created by this table. Green flowers and fruit splash the white glazed chintz cloth (matching green rough linen napkins are not shown). The earthenware plates are a gay design of pink roses and yellow daisies on white. The centerpiece, an oversized soup tureen on a tray of the same china pattern, sports an apple for its finial. Two antique porcelain cows are the perfect playmates for a pair of crystal duck-shaped wine decanters. A tailored silver flatware pattern, salt and pepper mill sets, and heavy crystal goblets finish the table.

# THE COLORED CLOTH

The magic of background color and pattern provides a whole new dimension in table setting design. Many of the tables in this book show a strong "pattern on pattern" feeling; others, a quiet harmony between the china and centerpiece arrangements and the design and colors in the tablecloth. Regardless of the approach, the colored and patterned cloth makes an interesting background for the display of objects. It can establish an entire mood for the setting.

## Luncheon in Sun Colors on a Terrace Coffee Table

Gaily-cushioned garden furniture and flowering plants turn any part of the terrace into a suitable dining area for informal entertaining in the summertime. Since there is so much color in the John Vesey furniture, only one of the sun colors—yellow—is used with cool black and white to form the color scheme for the table. The china pattern features a strong design in black and gold on its border. Vermeil flatware and accessories are used; and the egg-shaped bonbon box doubles as a sugar bowl for the mint iced tea, imaginatively served in oversized brandy snifters. The centerpiece is formed by a footed compote of lemon wedges decorated with yellow and white daisies. Yellow daisies carry the flower theme to each place setting, too. They are mixed with cigarettes in black basalt demitasse cups to provide the perfect decorative accent for the black and yellow scheme.

O utdoor dining—whether on the terrace, the patio, the sunporch, or even on a small balcony with the French doors thrown open—has become a favorite American custom. More and more summer entertainment is planned al fresco, providing unlimited opportunities for imaginative table arrangements that run the gamut from the most informal to the most formal in feeling. Whether a hostess follows period coordination or departs from it outrageously; whether she blends colors or clashes them; whether she uses fresh artichokes and mimosa in the center, or trails ivy through the decanter; whether she serves mint iced tea in brandy snifters or makes decanters into flower vases; whether she sets places on a bare table top or mixes striped and flowered linens with abandon, outdoor dining seems to provide the time and place for creating a fresh, individual look.

# OUTDOOR DINING

John Vesey's sunny garden becomes the scene of a festive Sunday luncheon. The large reproduction eighteenth-century Strasbourg faïence plates with their bold cabbage rose design are set off dramatically on the rough wood table. The centerpiece, a white glazed bowl shaped like a cabbage, contains an artichoke on a bed of lemons and oranges, and circling the bowl is a garland of fruits and vegetables. Napkins of rough beige linen trimmed in white are used, along with sterling salts and peppers in a watermelon pattern and a simple contemporary flatware pattern. Sterling porringers serve as ashtrays, and sterling jiggers as cigarette urns. Notice the larger water tumblers, the oversized burgundy glasses, and the white wine glasses—in reality, liqueur glasses. This imaginative use of crystal adds a note of informality to the setting. And, to reinforce the whole theme of a gay party, the *trompe l'oeil* chairs are satires of wooden buckets, complete with painted monkey, fox, and curious dog.

*Sunday Lunch*

*on a Wormy*

*Chestnut Table*

# Dessert for Two in the Moonlight

The typical male cry of "I like to see what I'm eating!" is quickly dispelled by this romantic setting in a garden illuminated by a single candle and a full moon.

The table setting is in keeping with the mood of a warm summer's night. A design of butterflies fluttering in various shades of green grass is printed on a circular organdy cloth. Brilliant-hued flowers decorate the earthenware dessert plates, and flowers also hatch forth from the sterling silver egg box at each place. An ivy plant in a sterling cigarette urn trails unabashedly through the hole in the center of a crystal decanter filled with apricot brandy.

An ivory-handled snuffer rests on the table, as part of the decoration—but ready to snuff the flame in the old-fashioned sterling candlestick.

A hand-engraved sterling flatware pattern and the simplest of liqueur glasses complete the setting.

# Dinner on the Terrace

## Overlooking Central Park

Dessert is served on a New York terrace overlooking the cool trees of Central Park in a setting of simple design, with a graceful balance of gleaming silver, crystal, and green-on-white china. The white terrace furniture is a perfect foil for this predominately white setting. The china, with its raised green leaf pattern, an eighteenth-century English reproduction, is combined with silver flatware of contemporary lines, an English sterling reproduction coffee set, goblets of deeply-cut parallel lines, and a centerpiece that is both useful and decorative. The sterling tray of the hurricane lamp is filled with fresh daisies, and no city breezes can extinguish the candle's flame protected so nicely by the gracefully-shaped glass bell.

MRS. CHARLES W.
ENGLEHARD
*Tiffany Hostesses' Show*

## Dinner for Four on a Formal Terrace

Mrs. Charles W. Englehard designed her dinner for four on a city terrace to set off her cane-backed chairs and her white tablecloth embroidered with silk cabbage tulips in pink and rose. The centerpiece is an etched glass hurricane lamp, twenty-two inches tall, over her telescopic vermeil candlestick—an idea guaranteed to survive terrace or air-conditioner breezes. Mrs. Englehard chooses bone china heavily decorated in gold and pink roses and an equally detailed vermeil flatware pattern. Richly cut goblets contrast with antique salt dishes of plain enameled white porcelain. The table ornaments are an assortment of vermeil ashtrays and urns and two antique boxes, one in gold and one in vermeil.

There is a studiously cluttered look about this table; Mrs. Englehard obviously delights in the effect of intricately patterned objects, and many of them.

William Baldwin has done this country luncheon in the unmistakeably courageous combination of hot Matisse colors. The Victorian Gothic rattan screen and tall plants sitting in straw baskets, lend an open, "terrace" feeling.

Even the linens sharply contrast in pattern and feeling. The tablecloth is a bright orange French cotton splashed with yellow flowers, while the napkins are of green and white striped crisp cotton. An informal blue and white flowered china pattern is used, with white porcelain-handled flatware. The heavy crystal goblets are cut with a swag motif. Accents of gold appear in the vermeil accessories, including an eighteenth-century German vermeil coffee pot in the Baroque style. Brightly colored anemones transform a crystal wine decanter into a vase, and further color is provided by a large round straw basket filled with fresh fruit. The folding straw and iron chairs have cushions of a French cotton print, yellow bamboo on black. The guardian of the scene is a large eighteenth-century Lowestoft dog, sitting calmly by the "Yucca Elephantipi" tree.

# Hommage
# à Matisse

BALDWIN & MARTIN INC.
*Tiffany Decorators' Show*

## Luncheon in a Summer House

WILLIAM PAHLMANN ASSOCIATES
*Tiffany Decorators' Show*

William Pahlmann has designed a terrace luncheon in cool summer colors of yellow, rose, and soft green. He carries forth his color scheme in the china, centerpiece, linens, and even in the furniture.

Luncheon is served on a patio with a terrazzo floor covering of white pebbles set into green marble tiles. Lemon yellow latticework screens and two towering green tree-plants in green jardinières frame the table. English Regency chairs in coffee-colored bamboo sport green plaid linen cushions. The simple yellow linen napkins on a rose linen cloth form the perfect background for the country earthenware with pink roses and green leaves on a white ground. The large soup tureen in the center of the table is ringed by a decorative combination of yellow mimosa and fresh green artichokes. A flatware pattern with a Gothic arch motif on the handles and traditionally cut goblets complete the setting.

# A "Special Occasion" Luncheon

## on a City Terrace

Eating out-of-doors does not imply that the setting has to have an informal look. Here the dessert course for a "special occasion" luncheon is set on a city terrace—and champagne will be served. The small white iron and glass-topped table provides a perfect background for a few impressive objects. A white shell dish, filled to overflowing with fresh fruit, is used as the centerpiece. The cachepot with its cabbage rose design, doubling here as an attractive champagne cooler, shares honors with the shell as the centerpiece interest. The dessert plates feature hand-painted designs of pastel flowers, part of an eighteenth-century English reproduction series of bone china. A handsome sugar sifter, shell ashtrays, and cigarette urns in sterling, a footed silver tray of petits-fours, and the most delicate of thin-stemmed champagne goblets lend an air of elegance to this outdoor setting. Pink felt place mats with a scalloped edge are used, with fine white linen napkins (not shown).

# THE PICNIC

ICNIC *is a term that usually denotes a family outing by a river or in the woods, complete with paper plates, potato salad, suntan lotion, and crawling ants. However, the joy of eating out-of-doors has increasingly stimulated hostesses to organize "picnics" in their back yards, in the garden, or even on their city apartment terraces, with a great deal more thought than the paper plate philosophy entails.*

*The picnic is also studied rusticity, which differentiates it from terrace dining. Color, pattern, and imaginative use of objects can transform a merely informal occasion into a charming still-life scene, as seen in these picnics designed by decorators.*

Mrs. Russell Davenport of McMillen Inc. has set a gay picnic on a green lawn under an umbrella made of a fabric splashed in Matisse colors to point up the color theme. There are two tables, one set for three with straw "Asian armrests" drawn up to them, and a smaller table for two using colored cushions for seats. The tablecloths, napkins, and cushions are a riot of purples, mauves, reds, and oranges, in plaids as well as solid colors. Straw picnic accessories, flatware with handles of white bone china, Mexican cotton napkins arranged in a porcelain rose (forming the centerpiece of the larger table), brightly colored plates with black dots, and the background of greenery make this picnic with a Côte d'Azur air to it seem very tempting indeed.

# Picnic in Matisse Colors

MCMILLEN INC. *Tiffany Decorators' Show*

# Picnic for a
# Sunday Painter

## MRS. HENRY PARISH II, INC.
### Tiffany Decorators' Show

Mrs. Henry Parish II sets a picnic for a Sunday painter, using an overall bright blue and white color scheme in conjunction with wicker. On a gaily striped canvas rug, she uses individual blue and white striped umbrellas attached to low-slung wicker chairs with cushions covered in blue or white. Blue and white figured china, polished wooden flatware, and other picnic accessories are set out on little round wicker tables. A latticework wicker screen entwined with greenery and a still-life painting resting on an easel with a painter's palette and brushes add to the atmosphere. The subject of the still-life by Laurance Tompkins is a group of hard-boiled eggs encased in a special egg-carrying round wicker basket, its open lid revealing a blue and white print lining. The model for the still-life lies on the table by the painting.

# THE CRYSTAL TABLE

*The sparkle and gleam of crystal has made it one of the most attractive art and decoration forms through the ages. Crystal catches and throws off light reflections; it acts as a screen for textures, a prism for color. In heavy, elaborate cutting patterns or with plain, undecorated surfaces, crystal has a primary quality of lightness and grace which is equally effective whether crystal is used exclusively or in combination with other elements.*

*The use of an all-crystal setting is an excellent way to feature an extremely colorful or patterned cloth or table top.*

Mimi Rand has combined crystal and faïence in "sea and earth" motifs on a table set for a seafood dinner. The cloth is a brilliant shocking pink, bordered in dark green and printed with life-sized lobsters of dark green. In the center of the table, between two pairs of tall crystal candlesticks, is a nineteenth-century faïence *choufleur* with a fat snail riding on top. Two eighteenth-century faïence leaf plates (Sceaux) and bunches of candied violet bouquets in crystal vases complete the centerpiece grouping. The crystal seafood servers, service plates, ashtrays, and goblets are cut in the same diamond pattern. Mrs. Rand chooses a very simple flatware pattern because of the strong pattern interest in the rest of the table.

## *La Folie en Rose*

MIMI RAND OF JESSUP-NEW YORK, INC.
*Tiffany Hostesses Show*

## The Summer Table

Everything on this fresh-looking table is in crystal, with the exception of the sterling flatware and salts and p ppers. The crystal is multipatterned: plain undecorated shapes for the plates, seafood servers, cigarette urns and ashtrays; a cameo pattern in the goblets; a candlestick shape based on sterling silver forms; a prism-cut bowl for the lemons, limes, and green leaves; a pair of paperweights shaped like acorn squash; and wine decanter with an oval-cut design and teardrop stopper. Even the crystal bell becomes a delicate *objet d'art* in this summery setting.

The crystal enhances the cotton place mats and napkins, printed with pink flowers and green leaves. An all-crystal table quite naturally calls for important design in the table linens.

# THE BUFFET

In modern times the buffet in America has become the most popular form of entertainment for three reasons: a lack of domestic help, a lack of house space, and the desire to entertain large groups of guests regardless.

The following settings show a variety of buffets, both formal and informal, as well as a clever use of room space to provide serving and seating areas for guests.

Tiffany designed this after-theater buffet in the home of Mr. Churchill Brazelton—whose small Manhattan apartment is jewel-like and boasts a terrace. There is no dining room, nor is there room in an apartment of this size to set up special tables, so the hostess must use her ingenuity to get the most from every bit of available space.

Here the radiator and window sill are pressed into service to form the serving table. A felt runner covers the radiator; two cupid sculptures and a pair of candlesticks are the only table decorations. The salad is arranged in a handsome cut-crystal punch bowl, hot croissants are served in a pierced silver basket, and a chafing dish keeps the artichoke hearts with mushrooms thoroughly hot. Some of the guests sit down at the library table, made over into a dining area. An elaborate gold and white tureen and tray form the centerpiece of the table; and equally elaborate sterling flatware, dark red, gold and white china, and cut-crystal goblets are used. Other guests are seated around the room on the divan and in chairs with small buffet tables drawn up to them.

Dessert is a separate entity and is served from the other end of the room, where a handsome black Louis XV commode becomes a table for the occasion. A different flatware is used for the dessert service—here it is vermeil, instead of sterling. All of the serving pieces are also in vermeil, to blend with the extraordinary eighteenth-

*The Elaborate Buffet in a Small City Apartment*

century vermeil épergne and the golden bronze candelabra. The strawberry ice-cream mold, decorated with large fresh strawberries, and the gay petits-fours are served on dessert plates of pale green and gold bone china. Champagne is served on the neighboring Louis XVI table. The glasses are a very elaborate Renaissance-looking champagne goblet pattern, and the wine itself is cooled in a gold and white porcelain cachepot.

After-dinner coffee means that everyone moves out on the terrace. Silver candlesticks with glass bells of every possible size, to protect the flames from the wind, are used everywhere as the sole illumination of the romantic terrace. The lights of the Manhattan skyscrapers provide background interest and contrast behind the marble statues on the wall, which originally graced European gardens. Coffee is served from a biggin (a reproduction Queen Anne silver pot on its warmer) into gold and white demitasse cups. To the right, on another table, is a tray of liqueurs ready to be served from two very differently cut crystal decanters.

As the wife of a prominent actor on Broadway, Mrs. Fonda entertains often after the theater. She likes to do it informally, while retaining a feeling of richness and ornamentation in her settings. The major interest in this green and gold buffet party is the unusual seating arrangement. Only one small round conventional table is used, and this so small it can only seat three, an interesting number for any table. Again, three people are seated on a three-sectional green silk pouf, and a small buffet table is drawn up to each guest. Champagne cools in a silver bowl behind them. The antique Venetian wicker bench, formerly used as a seat, is transformed for this party into a table for four; low footstools with gold cushions are drawn up to make seats.

Mrs. Fonda's setting also shows her Venetian background in her love of the ornate, as seen in the serving table. The cloth is of emerald green silk, heavily embroidered in gold, and she chooses all vermeil holloware and flatware to complement it. The plates are green and white, heavily encrusted in gold.

To repeat the flower theme on the serving table, the hostess places an occasional daisy on the seated tables. A butterfly perches on the center pyramid of fresh fruit and large daisies.

# After the Theater Buffet Supper

MRS. HENRY FONDA
*Tiffany Hostesses' Show*

# A Musical Buffet

This buffet supper before a concert or opera has been set up in the living room, using a musical theme throughout in the decorations and even in the china pattern. The hostess has utilized her pieces of furniture in their regular places, transforming the room into a comfortable serving and seating area. The meal is a typical Hungarian supper, featuring goulash and complete with the proper beverage for such a meal—beer—which is nicely chilled in an ice-filled silver bowl.

On the serving table two stately three-armed candelabra flank an antique black and gold lacquered musical instrument. The salad is kept crisp by placing the salad bowl in a larger crystal punch bowl filled with ice. The food is served in interesting silver shapes: the dark bread in a graceful basket; the salt rolls in a small sterling sports trophy.

Flanking the serving area is a square gaming table which is used to seat four; a low round coffee table in front of a settee also has places for four. Each small table used for seating guests has a toy gilt musical instrument as its centerpiece, and the plates have designs of antique musical instruments in browns and beiges on a white ground with gold rims. Notice the tall, graceful beer glasses which, in this setting, assume an air of formal elegance.

# The Strong-Patterned Buffet

### MRS. HENRY PARISH II, INC.
*Tiffany Decorators' Show*

Harmony and synthesis are achieved in Mrs. Parish's buffet through her selection of china, tablecloth, and centerpiece. A round circular white linen cloth falling to the floor has embroidered upon it strong accents of green ferns, leaves, and mushrooms. The china pattern matches the linens in feeling with its design of raised green leaves on white, a famous eighteenth-century English pattern still being manufactured today. The Georgian silver candlesticks, the taper stick, the English flatware, the child's cup used as a cigarette urn, and the creamer and pap boat used as sauce servers are all antique silver pieces. Two handsome cut-crystal decanters used to hold white and red wine are placed on pierced silver coasters. The centerpiece decoration is a handsome, yet simple-to-arrange, design of two compotes in the china pattern placed one on top of the other and filled with colorful fruits, leaves, and mushrooms.

82

# Before the Game Buffet

Felt—inexpensive and effective for special occasions—is here appropriately used for an autumn buffet with a football game in mind. Favors of felt footballs, mounted on satin ribbon in the colors of the favored team, become boutonnières to pin on lapels.

Cut-out felt leaves in browns and greens lie on a beige felt tablecloth. Swags of cones and autumn flowers mark the back edge of the table. The china pattern has a leaf decoration, and even the cookies in the pierced silver basket have an autumn leaf air about them. Hot punch is served from a handsome sterling punch cup set of a contemporary design. The flatware and dessert platter are also contemporary in feeling. A reproduction Queen Anne pot with its own alcohol warmer keeps the coffee piping hot.

# The Pink Party Buffet

The idea behind this setting—a delightful wedding, anniversary or birthday idea—is to coordinate the color of the china with the rest of the table. In this case, the pink, rose, and white of the reproduction eighteenth-century armorial plates are repeated in the napkins, the flowers, and the festive winding satin streamers.

The graceful bouquet of pink, rose, and white flowers fills an antique pierced silver basket. An added touch of harmony: the streamers on the table repeat the winding movement, as well as the color, of the ribbon motif on the border of the plates.

## The Cocktail Buffet

This cocktail buffet, by virtue of the large variety of serving pieces and glassware which create a happily jumbled effect, does not need a centerpiece. There is great variety and pattern on the table, but the setting is first and foremost *functional*. The mélange of elements has no underlying theme; rather each element is an attractive object in itself.

A tray holds bottles of liquors and various crystal decanters, each one tagged with a silver label denoting its contents. The cocktail napkins are tucked into a sterling basket-woven cachepot. An ice bucket with tongs, double jigger, martini mixing set, cocktail shaker, and turtle boxes for cigarettes provide strong accents of sterling silver. The pattern in crystal is varied, including heavy oversized old-fashioned glasses, traditional stemmed cocktail glasses, an ornately-cut basket, as well as simpler shapes. Italian *grissini* (breadsticks) rest in a tall tumbler; wafer crackers in the crystal basket; fresh radish roses and carrot sticks with parsley on the three-tiered silver compote. Onions blanketed in cheese are held with sword-shaped hors d'oeuvres picks; stuffed celery stalks are arranged in an oval crystal bowl, and assorted watercress sandwiches on a silver platter. Containers for the fruit, olives, and cherries for the cocktails, and for salted nuts to tease the appetite, complete this cocktail buffet table.

# THE CONTEMPORARY LOOK

Cherry blossoms and pussy-willows in a trifoliate sterling bowl make a simple Japanese arrangement for the centerpiece that repeats the flower motif in the contemporary china pattern. Sterling ashtrays that match the bowl, salts, and oddly-shaped peppers combine with a simple scroll-motif flatware and heavy Swedish crystal goblets. The gray linen tablecloth and rose linen napkins pick up the colors of the flowers in the china and center arrangement.

## The Oriental Look

# The Gray
# and Yellow Table

Around table is covered with a rough lemon-yellow linen cloth to harmonize with the gray-upholstered Paul McCobb chairs for this modern dining room. A strong Victorian pattern in china of black on white takes on a gray cast—an optical illusion. Black and white small-figured cotton napkins in sterling napkin rings look as if they were designed just for the china. The crystal goblets are simple in form, and all of the silver has a contemporary look by virtue of its plain surfaces and sharp angles. The candlesticks are low double funnels, while the salts, peppers, and lighter are a series of trapezoid shapes. Five-sided sterling ashtrays match the centerpiece bowl, which holds a pyramid of lemons. The fruit unifies the setting, matching the tablecloth in color accent to an otherwise all-gray scheme.

# Luncheon in a Small Contemporary Dining Room

An interesting blend of contemporary furniture by Dunbar and table accessories highlights this luncheon setting in a small dining room. The pale wood table is shaped into a curving rectangle, and with it are chairs covered in a blue and green plaid Thai silk. Matching fabric is used for napkins.

The all-white china pattern is decorated with layers of scallops on its edges. Sharp, angular crystal bowls, filled with eggplant, lemons, limes, and grapes, form the centerpiece. A contemporary vase serves as a breadstick container. The white wine decanter and the tall, majestic goblets further accentuate the modern feeling in the setting, as do the simple shapes of the sterling holloware. The reproduction early English flatware pattern as always fits smoothly into a twentieth-century table.

J oseph Lombardo has designed a make-believe Japanese "six-mat room" for his setting of dinner for three. A newly married Japanese couple is entertaining their first guest from the West. In this oriental decor, the eighteenth-century look transcends into a contemporary feeling.

The black-red lacquered rattan-on-wood low table is the central focus of the room. Three olive-green silk pillows with gold tassles are drawn up to the table, with a gold brocaded armrest at each place. Vermeil accessories are used with reproduction oriental Lowestoft plates decorated in Chinese red. Fish-shaped salts and peppers, shell ashtrays, and a bud vase holding a single yellow rose is used at each place. The Westerner has white and gold porcelain-handled flatware; his host and hostess, traditional chopsticks.

On the table lies a pair of turtles, symbols of good luck in the new marriage. Hot scented yellow napkins lie in crystal dishes at each place. Three bamboo candlesticks line one side of the gold-accented black table.

The room is lighted by two black lacquer and white parchment floor lanterns. A large red lacquered bowl filled with ice cools champagne for the Western guest.

# Japanese Bride and Groom
# Entertain Guest from the West

JOSEPH LOMBARDO INC.
*Tiffany Decorators' Show*

# Dinner on a Card Table

William Raiser's small apartment in New York is the setting for this dinner on a card table. The atmosphere is contemporary, the shapes are simple, and the setting seems to fit cozily with the important decor accents of a modern painting and a library of books.

The floor-length cloth is made of bright green felt, a warm background for the snow-white dinner china and the contemporary sterling flatware. Napkins are of cocoa-brown linen. The colorful fruit in the center crystal bowl is repeated in the vermeil boxes shaped like pears and oranges. The crystal stemware is tulip-shaped, repeating the gentle curves of the candlesticks—so delicate that the candles seem almost to be suspended in mid-air. Woven silver salt cellars at each place are used with a single oversized pepper mill. The silver lighter and cigarette box move from the cocktail table to the dinner table, along with individual crystal ashtrays, and back again after dinner.

When dinner is over, the card table disappears, and the small table holding the crystal champagne cooler once again stands beneath the painting.

## The Contemporary Table

A table and chairs with round shapes and bright color accents are a perfect adjunct to a contemporary house. The white pedestal table and shell chairs by Eero Saarinen of Knoll Associates, with seat pads of magenta and orange twill, are as important to this setting as the table elements. Vivid contrasts are everywhere—white, orange, and magenta with black. An all-white china pattern with plates in an unusual coupe shape is set off strikingly on circular place mats of heavy orange linen, and accompanied by a modern flatware pattern. The selection of crystal adds spice to the setting: vin rosé is served in oversized champagne glasses, and water in tulip-shaped wine goblets. Two slender candlesticks of different heights and pale green grapes in an oversized brandy snifter form the asymmetrical centerpiece. The bright colors of the linens and chair seats are picked up in the centerpiece of button flowers nestling in a black basalt bowl. This black touch is repeated in the demitasse cup, turned cigarette urn for the occasion, and ashtray.

# THE ONE-PATTERN SCHEME

Mrs. Nathaniel P. Hill has set a luncheon on a bare table in an eighteenth-century fashion. By using a minimum of elements, she emphasizes the china and crystal patterns. The flowered china is an excellent reproduction of a famous old German pattern. The center tureen is topped by a lemon finial; the smaller tureens, by apricot finials. The wine decanters and matching goblets for water and for white and red wine are cut in deep curving lines. A pair of vermeil salts and peppers and fine white linen napkins (not shown) complete this setting. There is an attractive freshness to the table, achieved by the concentration on the flower and fruit decoration on white china, as well as by the added touch of green in the white wine goblets.

*Luncheon*

*on a Bare*

*Table*

MRS. NATHANIEL P. HILL
*Tiffany Hostesses' Show*

# A Bare Table With Detail Interest

MRS. OGDEN L. MILLS *Tiffany Hostesses' Show*

Mrs. Ogden L. Mills has set her dinner table with an eighteenth-century feeling. Here, although the china pattern receives the obvious emphasis, there are many focal points to the setting, and a large amount of space is deftly utilized.

On an antique English table, Mrs. Mills uses china with a delicate blue-flowered pattern on white, a reproduction of an eighteenth-century design made originally for Frederick the Great; plain silver flatwear with pointed handles; reproduction George II candlesticks; and sterling reproduction ashtrays. The candlesticks and heavily cut goblets with unusual scalloped bases add formality to the setting. The covered tureen is decorated with a cupid aloft its finial. In the matching compotes on either side of the tureen, purple plums and strawberries introduce a strong note of color.

# The All-Over Patterned Look

Pattern on pattern is used with aplomb in this setting. The bold design of the tangerine, blue, and gold china blends into the beige cloth printed with white flowers. The traditional crystal stemware, the Georgian candlesticks, the ornate flatware—each element has its own strong pattern. Small bouquets of white flowers, clustered in cups around the centerpiece tureen, carry the patterned look still further.

# The Fern Table

VAN D. TRUEX
*Tiffany Decorators' Show*

Van Truex sets a table with a synthesis of elements; they are all in the same pattern. He imaginatively uses many shapes and sizes in one design of china—a very strong, ornate one at that, in the bold Imari colors of cobalt blue, tangerine, and gold. On the footed compotes in the center he places tangerines and strawberries to accentuate the colors of the china. Otherwise the whole centerpiece is a mass of delicate green fern, with plants placed disarmingly in small vase-urns and in the large center soup tureen.

Mr. Truex chooses vermeil flatware, candlesticks, and accessories to adhere to the Imari gold accenting the rest of the table. The total effect is not a crowded one; indeed, the graceful thinness of the fern removes any feeling of heaviness or exaggeration in this generous use of elements in one pattern.

# An Informal Luncheon

MRS. WILLIAM H. OSBORN *Tiffany Hostesses' Show*

Mrs. William H. Osborn has created a harmonious effect with a table full of gold and flowered porcelain. On round crocheted lace mats, she uses a china pattern with sprigs of pink and lavender flowers on white. The colors are repeated in the centerpiece, which consists of four matching cachepots filled with pink and lavender African violets, and in the pink linen napkins. A vermeil coaster for the bottle of white wine and vermeil holloware and flatware combine with undecorated crystal to give a shining gold accent to the informal luncheon setting.

# EIGHTEENTH-CENTURY INFLUENCE

## *A Dinner Predominantly White*

MRS. MUNN BAKER *Tiffany Hostesses' Show*

Mrs. Munn Baker sets a dinner table for four in white, with touches of café-au-lait. The centerpiece, an eighteenth-century Meissen white porcelain covered tureen, is placed on a white organdy tablecloth delicately embroidered with carnations, and is surrounded by four antique Berlin porcelain candlesticks. To complement her tureen, Mrs. Baker chooses an eighteenth-century reproduction white china with hand-painted pink flowers decorating the centers. She combines her antique fish knives and forks with an English reproduction flatware of the same design. The goblets for water and white wine are in a simple pattern, and Mrs. Baker uses brandy snifters for the red wine goblets.

The hostess is also a pepper lover. One kind is served in an antique silver shaker, another in a silver mill; with them she uses eighteenth-century Meissen salt dishes that are a perfect match for the dinner plates. The dinner menus are written on her own white Staffordshire menu stands. Silver ornaments on the table are four antique ashtrays with coins in the centers and four eighteenth-century chased cigarette boxes.

The caramel color in the silk seats of the cane-back Louis XV chairs is repeated in the unusual fleur-de-lis grospoint rug made by Mrs. Baker. The rug is not shown in the photograph, but it is an important color accent to this white setting.

# A Dinner in Classic Simplicity

GLADYS FREEMAN *Decorations Editor,* TOWN & COUNTRY

Miss Gladys Freeman has set an understated table in the eighteenth-century tradition. The emphasis is on balance and proportion, both of shape and of decorative motif. The centerpiece is a classic silver footed tureen with a berry finial; flanking it are two pairs of Queen Anne reproduction candlesticks. The silver flatware is a seventeenth-century reproduction with pistol-handled knives. The central focus is on the dinnerware—faithful copies of the Chinese Lowestoft armorial crest plates which were so popular in that era. The warm oranges and reds of these plates are the only color keynotes to this subdued setting. The crystal is also eighteenth-century in inspiration with its air twist stem, but a twentieth-century addition are the dotlike bubbles on the bowls of the goblets.

Miss Freeman uses her own beautifully embroidered écru linens in this Louis XVI dining room.

# TV Dinner for Two

MRS. ARTHUR
HORNBLOW, JR.

*Tiffany Hostesses' Show*

Mrs. Arthur Hornblow, Jr., has set a TV dinner for two on individual tables, combining a very modern entertainment medium with a traditional French setting. Her colors are mauve, pink, and blue, with touches of gold. She places mauve china with a gold border on place mats embroidered with pink and blue flowers. White wine is chilled in a sterling wine cooler kept on a side table; the other side table holds a Directoire-inspired coffee set, decorated with tiny roses on a gold border. An attractive splash of pattern results from a combination of the blue satin-covered Louis XV chairs, the hand-painted silk screen with blue and white Provincial figures, the antique rose octagonal patterned rug, and two different designs of china.

In direct antithesis to the period French furniture are the very contemporary brass and white marble buffet tables—and, of course, the television set facing the chairs.

A china pattern is the unifying theme of this setting in a harmonious blend of honey beiges and blues. The strong blue decoration on the pale gray ironstone is an exact reproduction of an Early American pattern, even to the heraldic shield in the center. The covered tureen on its tray with a silver ladle inside is used obviously not only as a food container but also as the centerpiece focal point; the decanters of the red and white wine are important accents to the center decoration. Creamers from the coffee set serve as charming small vases for the yellow, blue and white flowers. The cigarette urns and ashtrays in sterling are contemporary, yet they fit in perfectly with the simplicity of the late seventeenth- and eighteenth-century English flatware and American ironstone. Since there is strong pattern interest in the china and in the heavy embroidered linen tablecloth and napkins, the crystal and silver on this table are simple in shape and in detail. The warm beige of the linens is an excellent background for almost any color scheme.

*An Early American Table*

## An Eighteenth-Century French Table

This eighteenth-century table in a French mood literally sparkles with pattern and design. If this setting were laid on a tablecloth with a pattern of its own, the whole setting might lose itself in a morass of detail. But here, against a highly polished wood background, a vigorous harmony is achieved with flowers, fruit, ferns, intricately cut crystal, and elaborately decorated vermeil flatware. The lavenders, roses, and yellows of the Strasbourg reproduction plates and matching tureen are repeated in the faïence fruit used as decoration on the table. The vermeil flatware and holloware further accent the yellow color, and a feeling of coolness is supplied by fresh green fern plants in cachepots.

Every element on this table is a reproduction of eighteenth-century forms. The china pattern is based on the old French "Chantilly" design, with a crisp decoration of blue carnations on white—and to match the plates, a covered tureen and tray centerpiece and chinoiserie figure salts and peppers. The sterling flatware with its pistol-handled knives is reproduction English; the ashtrays are copies of the "Armada" silver designs, fashioned by the English from captured Spanish silver. The sterling tea caddy, Queen Anne candlesticks, sugar sifter (formerly used as a powder dredge for powdering wigs), and crystal goblets are all reproductions from English originals.

# An Eighteenth-Century Dinner

# Dining Before the Opera

DIANE TATE & MARIAN HALL INC. *Tiffany Decorators' Show*

On a round table a musical dinner is arranged by Marian Hall of Tate & Hall. The furniture is placed on a black needlepoint rug with a vigorous design of bright flowered squares. The elements of the table are delicate by contrast.

Fawn-colored musical instruments decorate the center of the gold-rimmed white china. The shell-motif flatware is in vermeil, as are all the table accessories, including the centerpiece candelabra-bowl filled with a mass of red roses and purple violets. The goblets feature a rich gold etched design of grapes on their rims. A circular white embroidered organdy cloth is placed over a pink satin base, with the resulting effect of bathing the setting in a rosy light. Still in a musical mood, a pair of eighteenth-century gilt wood Italian appliqués of tambours flank the silver and gilt wood central design of a violin. Even the chairs—gray and orange lyre-backs with cane seats in the French Directoire manner—carry out the musical motif.

113

# EXECUTIVE LUNCHEONS

*Luncheon*

*in a*

*Board Room*

Time & Life Building

Luncheon for six executives is set in one of the board rooms in the new Time & Life Building. The oval table of ebony with a walnut edge is the perfect backdrop for the red, gold, and white color scheme of this setting. All of the sterling flatware and holloware pieces are in golden vermeil, and the gold color is repeated in the rim of the china pattern. The accessories are an assortment of textured objects in a basket-weave design. The center basket-bowl, riding on the back of a crawling turtle, is filled with maps of the world. Flanking it are a pair of basket-woven cachepots, used to hold Time Inc.'s magazines, while a differently shaped cachepot serves as a pencil mug. The tall water goblets are chalice-shaped. A coffee service is placed on the white marble-topped black cabinets. (The sterling coffee pot has its own warmer—an important factor in a long lunch hour.)

Bright red linen napkins match the bright red felt contemporary chairs, and a bouquet of red carnations and daisies in the corner repeats the color accents.

Luncheon is being served in an executive's corner office in the new Time & Life Building. The working tools of the desk have been cleared off, with the exception of the telephone, yellow pads, and magazines under discussion. There is a concentration of heavy crystal and simple, functional shapes in silver and china. A contemporary white china pattern featuring coupe-shaped plates is combined with a plain silver flatware pattern and crystal tumblers weighing two and one-half pounds each. Smaller matching tumblers are in reality cocktail glasses, but serve nicely here as pencil holders. One large square silver box for cigarettes and one large round silver ashtray take care of the smoking needs of the threesome. Each executive has his own sterling coffee service to avoid the passing back and forth of the coffee pot through the meal. A three-tiered sterling compote stand serves as a useful centerpiece to hold the sandwiches, potato chips, and relish.

The Thai silk green and blue plaid napkins harmonize with the green and blue plaid contemporary chairs and lend a pleasant color accent to this office setting.

# *Luncheon at an Executive's Desk*

*Time & Life Building*

# THE WEDDING ANNIVERSARY

*Dinner in Gold and White*

A table all in vermeil is set in the yellow and gold French dining room of Mrs. Edward Bigler.

The white marble top of the gold and white Louis XV table is inlaid with designs of the sea. The marine theme is carried out in the vermeil accessories: tiny shell boxes, shell cigarette urns, and a jeweled 18-carat gold lighter by Schlumberger in the shape of a flexible fish. The vermeil centerpiece bowl, flanked by a pair of Georgian candelabra, has in its center a cupid basking in a variety of yellow and white flowers. A rich design in gold covers the bone china dinner plates. matched in feeling by the vermeil flatware design.

Tate & Hall have designed a Golden Anniversary dinner of classic simplicity, yet the effect is one of great elegance and richness. A table in a charming mixture of sun colors has been set against a background of gilt petitpoint antique French chairs. A very deep yellow silk skirt underlies the sheer white embroidered cloth, creating an illusion of burnished gold. Bone china in tangerine and gold on white rests on vermeil service plates, and the most ornate of vermeil flatware patterns contrasts with the simplest of slender crystal goblets. Peach and gold-colored carnations are arranged with dark green leaves on a series of vermeil compotes.

## *The Golden Anniversary Dinner*

DIANE TATE & MARIAN HALL, INC. *Tiffany Decorators' Show*

# *Silver Anniversary Party*

## *in Shades of Gray*

The twenty-fifth wedding anniversary is marked in this chiaroscuro table set in Princess Gourielli's gray, black, and white dining room. The table, covered with a fine gray and white embroidered cloth, is accented formally with silver objects. The four-light Queen Anne style candelabra and an assortment of silver boxes, tea caddies, cups, and other shapes in silver—collected through one's married life—decorate the center of the table. Dominating this setting is a massive silver bowl with montieth edge, filled to overflowing with packages wrapped in shiny silver paper and tied with silver ribbons— gifts for the anniversary couple. One slender crystal candlestick rises from the center of the bowl, holding a conical abstract made of silver ribbon. A handsome dark gray and white china pattern is used with the finely etched crystal and silver flatware.

This lightheartedly formal table contrasts the polished gleam of silver with the warmth of sandalwood and the off-white of the informal cotton print tablecloth.

Silver shapes are set off to perfection against the gray and white fabric. An undecorated Norfolk Isle pine, surrounded by four mint-filled shell dishes, rises majestically from a sterling silver urn between two Queen Anne style four-light candelabra. The mixture of pine and tall tapers lends an impression of height to this table. Two antique dolphins made of rams' horns with sterling silver heads and tails twist playfully around small bouquets of mignonette at either end of the centerpiece.

Sterling silver gadroon and leaf-bordered service plates with matching bread and butter plates and salts and peppers combine with flower-handled flatware and the plainest of cigarette urns and ashtrays to provide the more formal elements of the setting. Intricately cut stemware picks up the pattern in the cloth.

Many periods of silver are successfully used on this table, proving that good basic designs from any era may often be mixed.

*Silver Anniversary Dinner on a Cotton Cloth*

# The Bride

# Cuts

# The Cake

MRS. CHESTER BURDEN

*Tiffany Decorators' Show*

Mrs. Chester Burden of the Burden Littell Bureau sets a wedding table to honor the traditional cutting of the cake and toasting of the couple in champagne. Her party is a montage of pink and green sherbet colors. Pink satin lines the antique cloth of mull embroidered in écru lace daisies. Fresh green smilax winds around the bottom of the large, four-tiered, flower-crowned wedding cake, elaborately frosted with pink roses and lily-of-the-valley. A fountain of pastel and white flowers flows down from the bobèches of each of the rococo Georgian silver candlesticks, matching the flowers adorning the cake. A bridal bouquet of white flowers and pink roses, festooned with pink ribbons, lies on the table together with Mrs. Burden's antique ivory lace bridal handkerchief.

Pale pink and pale green dessert plates, decorated with gold, carry out the color scheme. The champagne glasses with an etched grape motif are the perfect match for the antique silver bowl with its raised relief of grapes on the rim, used to cool bottles of pink champagne. As an added romantic touch, the cake knife is tied with lilies-of-the-valley and pink satin ribbon.

# THE WEDDING

A very feminine setting in a bridal mood combines the delicacy of crystal with a dainty floral pattern in porcelain. Hand-painted pink and blue rosebuds rim the bone china plates. In the center two crystal swans, an ancient marriage symbol, glide out from a plant-filled cachepot decorated with rosebuds. A cameo-patterned goblet and four crystal candlesticks add to the airy lightness of the setting. The richly-decorated flatware and Georgian-inspired sterling salts and peppers repeat the wreath design of the china.

Even the flower-embroidered white organdy linens seem to be designed just for this setting—a table dedicated to the bridal or anniversary theme.

*A Wedding Luncheon*

# The Birthday Luncheon

What child wouldn't be delighted by this whimsical centerpiece, with its woolly monkeys romping hilariously on a candy-cane jungle gym that is beribboned and bedecked with gaily wrapped gifts? The ribbons are stretched to the corners of the table and held to the cloth by double-faced cellophane tape.

A pair of two-handled crystal loving cups hold bouquets of giant lollipops. Even milk takes on a party glamour when it is served in crystal mugs. A simple sterling flatware pattern fits into the festive scheme. The tablecloth, made for this occasion of bright yellow felt, provides the perfect background for the sparkle of red party favors.

An adult china pattern in a strong design of blue flowers and bugs on a white ground seems especially appropriate for the children here.

# THE

# BIRTHDAY

# PARTY

Andy Warhol has designed a deluxe birthday party for children in a riot of hot, clashing colors. The table is set in front of a "Pin the Tail on the Donkey" screen. The rug is splashed with cherry-red roses and green leaves, bordered in white tassels, and the same fabric is used on the high-backed cane chairs. This rose fabric is also used for the napkins on the round party table. The unusual cloth is made of basket-woven strips of white crepe paper and white ribbon, and is bordered with white tassels. Because children love the unusual, large serving spoons are used for ice cream, and each child has a different plate design. Ice cream is served in sterling silver porringers.

Large crepe paper favors are perched on chairs, and the table is a fascinating potpourri of shapes and colors. It is filled with brightly-wrapped packages, sterling silver sipper straws in coke bottles painted gold, a tall white birthday cake shaped like a silo, and two balloon-shaped glass "hat holders" crammed with multicolored candies.

*Birthday*

*Party for*

*Cornelia*

ANDY WARHOL
*Tiffany Decorators' Show*

125

# Birthday Buffet Luncheon on a Terrace

Summer in New York is not a hardship if one has a terrace—this one belonging to Princess Gourielli is transformed by Tiffany into a midsummer's-day dream of unusual shapes painted in pastel colors for a birthday party. A white wrought-iron plant holder is converted into the centerpiece—a veritable "birthday tree." The plants have been removed, and instead the branches hold either gay gifts or crystal and silver bowls filled with green and orange melon balls. A melon ball compotière continues the theme by forming the center decoration of the incidental side tables used for eating. A champagne fruit punch is served from a bowl on a separate table, and oversized crystal brandy snifters double as punch cups. A large, handsome silver tureen holds the main hot dish, and variety is the keynote throughout the holloware. On the serving table, for example, tailored sterling salts and pepper mills are used, but on each individual side table there is a pair of owl salts and peppers meditating over a pineapple-shaped ashtray. A seventeenth-century English reproduction sterling flatware is used, and the delicate china pattern—sky-blue flowers on a white ground—adds a further color accent to the scheme. The birthday cake, adorned with pastel flowered icing, and clusters of pastel balloons tied to fence posts and chair-knobs make this setting a refreshing, festive sight on a hot summer's day.

# THE CHRISTMAS TABLE

## Christmas Dinner Around a Crèche

MRS. HOWELL H. HOWARD *Tiffany Hostesses' Show*

Mrs. Howell H. Howard's Christmas dinner for eight is a symphony of pink, gold, and silver, designed to display her rare and beautiful seventeenth- and eighteenth-century Neapolitan crèche figures. She uses all vermeil service plates, holloware, and flatware on an antique gold and white table. The table is decorated by two center runners of pink foil with an overmat of silver lace, an inventive idea that is repeated in the wrapping of gift packages at each guest's place. Green smilax runs from the centerpiece to the corners of the table and winds garland-fashion around the table legs. Pink goblets on white stems carry out the color scheme of the holiday table. Mrs. Howard uses two Louis XV armchairs with oval backs at either end, and little gold chairs with Christmas-red velvet seat pads for the center seats.

The whole focus of her table lies in the centerpiece, where she has used the three separate polychrome angel groups heralding the Nativity. The angels, part of a crèche group made in eighteenth-century Naples, are most unusual museum pieces. The large angel in the center group, who is depicted appearing to the humble shepherd and his flock, is dressed in rich robes of silver and gold-embroidered satin. To lend a more festive air, a leafy background dotted with tiny gold twinkling lights has been constructed for this and the adjacent angels.

*Norfolk Pine*

*Christmas*

*Table*

*Centerpiece*

The circular shape in crystal, silver, and red is repeated in this predominately crystal table. The galaxy of round shapes includes the contemporary Swedish candlesticks—three pairs of different sizes and shapes; the large, crystal, footed punch bowl holding the tree; the stemware in a rounded tulip shape; the liqueur glasses of the same pattern encircling the bowl, each glass crowned by a silver Christmas tree ornament, like a magic soap bubble; round dinner plates with their strong orange-red pattern on white; round sterling covered boxes and ashtrays; the round Directoire-inspired salt cellar; the silver table bell, and even the tiny silver and red Christmas balls dotting the branches and base of the Norfolk pine.

Variety is achieved by the strong vertical and horizontal accents which cut through the delightful circles: the Gothic soaring of the candles in their holders, the vertical cutting of the center punch bowl and the goblet stems, the long, clean lines of the contemporary flatware pattern, the cross branches of the Norfolk pine, and the unexpected addition of silver and red bows on the branches of the pine and the outer edges of the tablecloth.

A clever *trompe l'oeil* device is shown here in a Christmas table designed on a parallel horizontal basis. A long table is divided into three lengthwise sections by parallel linen runners and a centerpiece row of white candles.

The linen runners, in Christmas colors of red and green, feature white circles with a center decorative motif, such as nuts or holly, over which crystal dinner plates are placed, creating an unusual effect. Crystal butter plates for croissants and heavy goblets are used. The contemporary flatware pattern harmonizes with the sterling candlesticks, the bases of which are filled with gay bouquets of white carnations, green leaves, and red berries.

# A Christmas Party with Crystal Plates

# THANKSGIVING

Mrs. Moss Hart has set a family Thanksgiving table in an Early American dining room, complete with a collection of pewter of the period. The furniture includes an Early American highchair for the smallest member of the family. The setting is centered around a symbol of the harvest—a wheat-filled pumpkin studded with large walnuts. Polished red and yellow apples on sterling silver compotiers encircle the pumpkin. Four dishes containing gum drops, peanut brittle, nuts, and raisins are placed on the table to add gaiety and color accent.

Mrs. Hart has used an iron stoneware pattern in the orange, yellow, and blue Imari colors, so appropriate for the holiday season. The china picks up the clear colors of her fruit-and-candy arrangement. With it she uses an ornate flatware pattern with mythological scenes in high relief on the handles, silver shell ashtrays, and tall silver salts and pepper grinders. The edge of the beige felt tablecloth has been scalloped with pinking shears, and with it Mrs. Hart uses heavy beige linen napkins. Following the tradition of the first Pilgrim Thanksgiving, she serves ale and cider, instead of wine and water, in heavy silver tankards—one size for men, a smaller one for the ladies. Baby is not excluded from the decorating scheme; he uses his own mug and flatware, together with a matching dessert plate in the stoneware pattern for his main course.

Vegetables symbolic of the harvest decorate the display of pewter on the sideboard and shelves.

# Thanksgiving Dinner for Six and One-Half

MRS. MOSS HART
*Tiffany Hostesses' Show*

# THE EASTER PARTY

The following settings of Easter tables in pastel colors are imbued with a look of freshness. The Easter symbols of the lily, the egg, and the rabbit have been imaginatively used to set the theme of the occasion.

## A Traditional Easter Table

Mrs. Sarah Jackson Doyle has designed a traditional Easter luncheon, all in green and white, in an eighteenth-century Chippendale dining room. The centerpiece is a fabulous silver épergne with six candle holders, which Charles Mellon gave to J. P. Morgan. Mrs. Doyle has filled it with white Easter lilies, and the five silver baskets attached to the épergne hold green and white mints. On embroidered white organdy place mats, the china pattern, featuring a florid dark green, ivory, and gold design, combines with the simplest of sterling flatware and crystal patterns. The slim-stemmed crystal repeats the delicate grace of the lily shape. Sterling salts and peppers with a Chippendale border motif, rectangular silver cigarette boxes, and an assortment of silver ashtrays complete the setting.

SARAH JACKSON DOYLE
*Tiffany Decorators' Show*

James Amster designed this Easter luncheon, using an oval eight-eenth-century Chippendale mahogany hunt table and Italian Directoire chairs with lyre backs. The seat pads are covered with a contemporary woven green fabric. Mr. Amster believes in combinations: he uses three different whites in linens and china; he combines the dark wood table with chairs in light wood; he uses both English and Italian furniture; he combines sterling silver and vermeil accessories. The linens are oatmeal-colored with green openwork embroidery. Stark white creamed soups rest on dinner plates of a bold gold-edged green leaf pattern on off-white. The Easter theme is announced in the unusual centerpiece: a boxwood (topiary) form sprayed with lacquer and shaped like a nest, filled with multicolored, jewel-studded Easter eggs. There are two side boxwood forms shaped like hourglasses and decorated with eggs and tiny white rosebuds made of starched cloth.

*An Easter Luncheon with Boxwood Centerpiece*

JAMES AMSTER
ASSOCIATES
*Tiffany Decorators' Show*

# Fête de Pâques—
## in Pink and Green

Valerian Rybar has designed an Easter party using spring colors and two familiar symbols of Easter —the egg and the rabbit—for his decorative scheme. Luncheon for eight is set on a long table placed on a rose and beige rug. Black and gold lacquered Sheraton chairs, their seats covered in a crisp apple-green silk, are drawn up to the table. The whole table is a harmonious blend of green with two shades of pink. Apple-green plates with pink flowered-design centers are used on a pale pink silk tablecloth with white polka dots. The napkins are of a deeper pink silk, also with white polka dots.

Mr. Rybar uses heavy cut-crystal goblets and an antique English flatware pattern in vermeil. All of the sterling accessories, from the trimmed

## VALERIAN S. RYBAR INC.
*Tiffany Decorators' Show*

crystal decanters holding vin rosé to the mustard pots, are in vermeil. At each guest's place, serving as a favor as well as a place card, is a vermeil egg box tied with pink velvet ribbon and pink flowers.

The pink and green Easter centerpiece consists of a three-tiered vermeil stand filled with light and dark pink eggs, field flowers, and greenery, flanked by two vermeil footed trays filled with the same arrangement. On each of the side trays one of Mr. Rybar's own antique porcelain bunnies nestles cozily amid the eggs and flowers.

# THE VALENTINE PARTY

*A Valentine's*

*Day Luncheon*

*for Four*

A cloth of pale pink felt covers this round table for a Valentine's Day luncheon. The small sterling heart-shaped frames serving as place cards at each place are favors for the guests on this festive occasion. A simple crystal vase holding three porcelain roses, the only centerpiece decoration, is surrounded by red felt hearts which are used as mats for the flowered porcelain ashtrays. A heart-shaped bonbon box is also placed on the table as additional accent. Delicate-stemmed champagne glasses keynote the "special occasion" feeling, and the Valentine theme is reemphasized by one crystal wine goblet filled with heart candies. The plates feature hand-painted fruits and flowers on a white ground.

139

# THE TEA PARTY

## *The Formal Tea Table*

This type of table provides the perfect opportunity to show off one's silver to its best advantage.

Queen Anne reproduction candelabra alternate with the contemporary round bowls filled with beaded spring flowers as the background decoration for the table. The flatware pattern, contemporary in feeling, combines perfectly with the Chippendale-bordered platters and with the Georgian reproduction skittleball kettle and coffee urn.

The tablecloth is heavy white linen with a gray design on white, a welcome relief from the usual plain white tea cloth. Since the cloth has such a strong pattern, a simple china design shows up to best advantage. Here the china features hand-painted fruits and flowers on a white ground; each plate carries a different design.

# An English Tea

MRS. EDGAR W. LEONARD *Tiffany Hostesses' Show*

The English tea means a wonderful cluttered look to the table, and the quantity and variety of delicacies served provides a great opportunity to use interesting objects from which to serve them.

Mrs. Edgar W. Leonard has designed her tea table as a symphony of blue with colorful accents supplied by the food (as, for example, fresh strawberries and varied jams) and by the vermeil holloware and flatware items. She uses a blue-on-gray stoneware pattern, utilizing many shapes of serving dishes and even odd pieces such as the tea caddy with its flower stopper. The tea napkins are printed in a gay blue and gold pattern; and blue, yellow, and white flowers fill the antique cachepot. Mrs. Leonard combines her antique vermeil cigarette urns and Regency flatware with contemporary vermeil, finding they all blend perfectly. The star of her table, however, is the cloth—of a most unusual 200-year-old écru batiste, embroidered with large figures depicting "The Cries of Paris." The pattern of this exquisite heirloom comes through in spite of the busy activity going on above it.

# The Uncluttered Tea Table

This setting has a dash of crème-de-menthe freshness in its emerald green, gold, and white theme.

A bone china pattern with green and gold fern decoration is featured on a small round table, set with tea sandwiches, buttered muffins, and angel cake.

The most important decorative accent is the cloth. White and green flowers are embroidered on a crisp white organdy circular skirt covering a white felt underskirt, thus echoing the color scheme of the china as well as lending an air of utter femininity to the table.

The round shape is the thing here—the sterling and china serving dishes and even the food repeat the magic circle. Flowers are not necessary on such a small table; the lemon and lime wedges match the table's basic color theme and supply the necessary decorative note of color. There is a balance of china and silver, very pleasing to the eye.

# THE HORSESHOW

*Horseshow Luncheon*

A bisque figurine, "The Hunter," by the American ceramic sculptor Edward Marshall Boehm, reigns supreme over the centerpiece decorations for this horsemen's table. Guarding it on either side is a line of sterling trophies of different sizes.

Forest-green place mats of heavy linen embroidered with white leaves and ferns set off the bright-colored "Hunt Scene" earthenware pattern. A flatware pattern with an architectural motif completes the overall theme of simplicity in this table.

# Maryland Hunt Cup Luncheon

BALDWIN & MARTIN INC.
*Tiffany Decorators' Show*

William Baldwin has designed a "Maryland Hunt Cup Luncheon" to honor a very important springtime event in the horse world. The traditional green and gold program of the hunt lies at each place, serving as a place card, and the handsome 1916 sterling Hunt Cup Trophy sits in the center place of honor. The decorative motif of large appliquéd lemons on a white linen cloth bordered in dark green, with matching napkins, is further accented by two crystal compotes on either side of the trophy containing lemons and leaves. White china with a border design of fluted waves is used with heavy, oversized cut crystal water tumblers and "rye-on-the-rocks" glasses. The English chairs are yellow-lacquered bamboo with seats covered in an unusual yellow and white paisley chintz.

# The Hunt Breakfast on a Kentucky Plantation

VALERIAN S. RYBAR, INC.

*Tiffany Decorators' Show*

Valerian Rybar has designed a sumptuous "after the hunt" feast in the dining hall of a Kentucky plantation. The setting is a dramatic blend of cherry red, bittersweet orange, dark wood, and silver.

The dining room has an eighteenth-century English flavor, and the antique mahogany table is accented with the symbols of the hunt. A large center sterling hunt trophy on a felt ribband base dominates the centerpiece, flanked by two massive sterling covered tureens. The base of the center trophy is decorated with stirrups and snaffles. Around the table six Georgian silver candlesticks are festooned with cherry and bittersweet felt decorations, centered with fox masks in rosettes and crossed by ivory-handled riding crops.

Armorial crest soft paste plates featuring cherry and bittersweet are used on sterling service plates with gadroon edges. Bittersweet linen napkins accompany round felt place mats, a bittersweet mat over a larger red one. Eighteenth-century English reproduction sterling flatware with pistol-handled knives is used.

An Adam Sheraton sideboard holds sterling hunting trophies, cigar boxes, and a large silver tray to serve the traditional bourbon mint juleps in sterling mint julep cups.

149

# THE FANTASY TABLE

This section is devoted to "fantasy" tables because—although it is usually impossible to duplicate the major emphasis of the setting in each case, whether it be a moonlit forest, a trompe l'oeil screen or a Russian onion-domed table—it is just such flights of fancy that set the creative mind at work.

## Supper on a Romantic Terrace

### DENISE OTIS AT RICHARD L. SANDFORT

Miss Denise Otis has designed a terrace dinner party for Tiffany, using a multicolored palette and focusing interest on her unusual centerpiece. Her "linens" of Thai silk, in interesting shades of greens, blues, and purples, have an iridescent glow in the candlelight. Shimmering Japanese gauze butterflies of all sizes hover over the white tapers and the large bouquet of bright paper flowers. The latter are executed in "The Morning Glory Fold," one of the important aspects of the art of Japanese paper folding. The graceful tulip-shaped crystal goblets and candlesticks add to the airiness of the setting. The bone china pattern has a design of pastel flowers, and is combined with a very simple sterling flatware pattern, silver fruits, and tiny mugs for cigarettes. In the background, champagne is cooled in a sterling basket-woven cachepot.

# Production Supper for "Redhead"

ROUBEN TER-ARUTUNIAN

*Tiffany Decorators' Show*

This supper-for-two setting represents a typical evening's work session for scenic designer Rouben Ter-Arutunian. The gifted artist did the sets and costumes for the Broadway hit, *Redhead*. The table is set for the dessert course in his studio—fruit, cheeses, coffee, candies and wine—on crystal plates, in pitchers, bowls, white glaze demitasse cups, and oversized glasses. Mr. Ter-Arutunian combines two patterns of sterling flatware and three patterns of crystal for his setting.

Nineteenth-century carved wooden chairs are pulled up to Saarinen's white marble pedestal table. These shapes against the dark parquet floor are accents of stark simplicity, emphasizing the atmosphere of a designer's studio. Amid the potpourri of the vestiges of a late evening supper are the tools of Mr. Ter-Arutunian's trade— swatches of fabric; sketches of costumes; drawing pencils in an antique porringer; the script of the book; and, most important of all, a scale model of the stage set, lighted from above by a metal work lamp.

153

# Dinner in a Tree House

**STEPHEN MALLORY
AND JAMES TILLIS**

*Tiffany Decorators' Show*

Mallory and Tillis have designed a unique dinner party for four. The setting, in a tree house high in the branches of a very lifelike tree, sparkles in a predominately blue and white color scheme. The wooden tree house and the contemporary shell-shape chairs and pedestal table with aluminum base are all in white. The decorators chose white dinner plates and a contemporary pattern of sterling flatware. The silver tumblers and heavy, oversized, crystal tumblers are for wine and water respectively. Blue and white linen napkins in sterling rings match the blue and white Chinese rice paper on the party favors at each place. The centerpiece is a rough piece of rock crystal, looking very much like a glacier formation. Champagne cools in a white glazed cachepot, and the straw basket on the right is filled with daisies and multicolored Japanese fans, in case the evening breezes do not suffice.

William Baldwin of Baldwin & Martin Inc. has created a luxurious setting for a bachelor's dinner.

The Spanish seventeenth-century dark wood table is set on a white goatskin rug. The dinner plate is of sterling silver, with matching butter plate. The bachelor's napkin is of the finest white linen, with his monogram in brown. Serving as table ornaments to delight his eye are an elaborate Georgian five-light sterling candelabrum; a large chased sterling tureen shaped into a lifelike reproduction of a seed-pod; owl-shaped mustard pot, and salt and pepper; and an artichoke box for cigarettes. Rather large goblets in a richly cut pattern and two silver pineapple menu holders complete the setting.

The red and white wallpaper-covered eight-panel screen and the matching fabric-covered chair provide a startling color accent.

The finishing touch of éclat: the diner's best friend—his dog—is represented here by a life-sized eighteenth-century Lowestoft hound, with a sterling porringer on a sterling plate in front of him.

# Dinner for One

BALDWIN & MARTIN INC.
*Tiffany Decorators' Show*

# Luncheon on a Tôle Table

MRS. T. REED VREELAND
*Tiffany Hostesses' Show*

Mrs. T. Reed Vreeland has done a fairy-tale setting that an imaginative hostess might adapt for terrace, sunroom, or summer garden. An old French dark green tôle table inspired by Byzantine design provides the important architectural unit. The table is topped by a lofty, canopied, onion-shaped dome on four supports, crowned with a finial of polished wood. It is set on a round carpet of green grass with four antique English beach chairs drawn up to it. The chair seats are covered in a fabric printed in a fresh black and white paisley design.

A vivid orange-red circular cloth of a heavy woven fabric covers the table, falling to the ground. Forest green napkins provide a strong color accent. An antique tôle and brass cachepot (a European five-liter measure) holding a palm makes the centerpiece of the table. The dessert china, which features a green leaf design on white, is a reproduction of an eighteenth-century English pattern. With it Mrs. Vreeland uses tulip-shaped goblets and silver accessories in vermeil: an elaborate flatware pattern, owl-shaped salts and peppers, the mustard jar in the shape of an owl with a field mouse in its mouth, and four sizes of boxes. Porcelain cigarette boxes and urns filled with pachysandra add decorative notes to a table that is alive with fun and fantasy.

# Manger à Trois

BRASWELL & COOK ASSOCIATES, INC.

*Tiffany Decorators' Show*

Braswell & Cook have constructed an elaborate dining room set which might have come from a Louis XIII shooting lodge.

A canopy on wooden posts and the back wall are covered in a deep sapphire-blue wool suede, with an important detailing of black piping. Side draperies of changeable violet taffeta are caught with black moire tiebacks. The floor is of gray, black, and white tiling in large squares, resembling the floors seen in the paintings of Flemish artists. Tall seventeenth-century chairs covered in a blue and white checked fabric are drawn up to the six-sided, oiled slate-top table on an aluminum base.

A large sterling tureen, sculptured in the shape of a many-petaled bud, is the centerpiece of the table. Large napkins of rough-textured linen printed in dark colors combine with dinner plates of a strong black and white pattern. Oversized water tumblers of cut crystal serve as red wine glasses, while smaller glasses of the same pattern are used as white wine glasses. The accessories, including the elaborate flatware and the artichoke box, are in vermeil. A bronze chandelier hanging from the canopy over the table shimmers in the light reflected by its rock crystal pendants and a large amethyst quartz piece shaped like an apple.

The console table is painted to look like lapis lazuli and white marble. The centerpiece flower arrangement of dried flowers in beige and toast colors is arranged in an antique blue Delft vase, and is dramatically illuminated. The console is set with a pair of crystal decanters for the red and white wine, a pair of antique hurricane lamps, and sterling demitasse cups with gold and white porcelain liners.

# Supper for Two in a Swan-Boat

STEPHEN MALLORY AND JAMES TILLIS
*Tiffany Decorators' Show*

The eight-foot-long white swan-boat used in this setting by Mallory and Tillis is the same type as those which, in another era, floated as decorations in the private lakes of Austrian nobles. The swan's neck is decorated with a garland of flowers; its harness is a pair of streamer ribbons. A small white table is covered with a filmy sea-green cloth embroidered in white flowers. Two small white chairs are drawn up to the table, which is set with sterling silver plates, finely etched champagne goblets, and a centerpiece of petits-fours on a silver bowl. A crystal hurricane lamp for illumination and a champagne cooler complete the table setting.

The decorators built a landing platform for the boat, as well as painting a lake-landscape backdrop in blue and white to give the illusion of an endless shoreline with trees and mist-shrouded ruins. Even suggestions of the river banks were built around the mooring, full of flowering white plants set in green grass.

# The Sitting

MRS. JOHN BARRY
RYAN III

*Tiffany Hostesses' Show*

Mrs. John Barry Ryan III has done a setting of an artist's studio that is a still-life in itself. The artist and the sitter have paused for a late lunch in a studio of a monotone mood, all in black and white and wood. An antique drawing table and stool are set on a paint-spotted canvas, against a white Moroccan screen, and a black tray with a tasseled cotton doily rests on the paintbox. A white bud vase and crystal paper weight add decorative accents.

A cane-back rocker, an antique wood table, and a *faux-bois* cabinet containing artists' materials in crystal and silver containers complete the furniture arrangement. The black and white patterned china combines with different patterns of crystal and black basalt for the serving of lunch. Fat silver turtles and silver vegetables recline on a zebra rug thrown on the canvas, and the model's silk kimono is tossed over the screen. To add further detail interest, white bisque shell containers are filled with sea shells and white chrysanthemums.

Both Mrs. Ryan's setting and that by Mr. Ter-Arutunian (page 152) are examples of the casual, unorthodox, and personal approach to relaxed, intimate dining—almost a "grab-bag" approach. They are full of unexpected personal objects—and ideas.

Mallory and Tillis have designed an after-dinner setting for a luxurious safari; their setting epitomizes the way to travel through darkest Africa in the greatest comfort. The guests are enjoying dessert, coffee and brandy on the finest crystal and golden vermeil, with a few eighteen-carat gold accessories thrown in for good measure— a far cry from rusticity.

A sand-colored burlap tent, trimmed in a darker shade of burlap piping, is gathered and slung from four tall eighteenth-century French palm trees made of gold-washed metal. The tablecloth, which matches the tent, completely covers a long narrow buffet. A giant hurricane lamp casts glowing candlelight over the crystal and gold.

The decorators have covered the floor with sand, to give an authentic desert air to the scene. A sedan chair of polished yew with burlap seat pads becomes a comfortable armchair when not being borne aloft by the native bearers. Additional seating space is provided by Austrian leather shooting stools. One of these stools, topped with a wooden tray, serves as a side table, complete with a vermeil bell to call for service. Desert grass grows around the gold palm trees, and the tent is filled with wicker traveling trunks, leather gun cases, pith helmets, and game bags.

# Safari

STEPHEN MALLORY
AND JAMES TILLIS
*Tiffany Decorators' Show*

163

# Soûper au Clair de la Lune

GENE MOORE *Tiffany Decorators' Show*

No nature lover could resist this romantic supper for two in the forest by the light of the moon. Gene Moore has set a table in a wooded glen, frosted with cobwebs and illuminated by moonlight, fireflies, and one candle. The ground is abloom with tiny green plants and succulents. A mint green color permeates the setting; it is the color of the felt seat pads for the black iron chairs, and of the underskirt beneath the sheer white embroidered cloth. The plates, too, have a pattern of this same green with gold. A vermeil candlestick, vermeil flatware, and a lacy-patterned crystal add sparkle to the table. Champagne cools in a heavy crystal cachepot, and a trio of vermeil owls—for salt, pepper, and mustard—hold conversation in the corner.

Even a lizard enjoys the scene from a chair, while a wise old owl gazes down benignly from the tree branch. Surely, at any minute, Puck will arrive to serve dinner.

## *The Seashell Luncheon*

Myriads of seashells of various sizes and shapes adorn this table for a seaside luncheon party. In the center, four white bisque shell compotes are filled with small flowering plants. Seashells are scattered over the sand-colored felt tablecloth with its scalloped edge; two large conchs made of white glazed bisque serve the same decorative purpose as a pair of tureens might do on a traditional table. White shell dishes for seafood are used on white shell-shaped dinner plates. The flatware has a shell as the only decoration on its handles, and even the sterling ashtrays and cigarette urns are shell-shaped.

166

# INSPIRATION OF THE SEA

Mrs. George F. Baker has utilized her lovely collection of antique silver and porcelain shells in this formal dinner setting. Her linens, of pale pink damask, with a deeper pink monogram on the napkins, provide the perfect backdrop for the pastels of the Chelsea shell groups. A large central group and smaller units of one and three of these delicate flowered shells are shown in the photograph. The large double clam-shaped dishes are antique English silver pieces. Mrs. Baker places an occasional cluster of pale pink carnations in crystal containers, and chooses white shell plates, cut-crystal goblets of a vertical design, and a reproduction English flatware pattern with pistol-handled knives. She uses the same white shell plates seen in the seashell luncheon (page 166), but the pattern assumes a much more formal aspect on this table.

*A Dinner*

*Using*

*Antique Shells*

MRS. GEORGE F. BAKER
*Tiffany Hostesses' Show*

# Yacht Club Party

WILLIAM PAHLMANN ASSOCIATES *Tiffany Decorators' Show*

Under a gay canvas canopy striped in sun colors, William Pahlmann has designed a dinner party at a yacht club, using a perfect seaside color scheme of blue-green and coral.

Covering the table is a circular skirt of coral chintz accented with blue-green linen napkins. The centerpiece, a large white bisque shell, is filled with tropical plants and flowers in coral and blue shades. The seashell plates are of white glazed bisque and the marine motif is also carried out in sterling shell ashtrays and a flatware pattern with handles sculptured with waves and shells. At each place an antique white porcelain hand holds a shell filled with anthurium and leaves.

# THE BIRDS AND SPRING FEVER

One of the most decorative additions to any home is the porcelain bird. The traditional sanctuary for these lifelike figurines is the hall table, the mantelpiece, or the bookcase shelf.

The following settings show how porcelain birds on the table can enhance the fresh, springlike look of the setting, no matter what the color combinations of the linens, flowers, fruit centerpieces, or china patterns. Some of the settings use birds as the central focus of the decorating plan; others add one or two as a corollary to the major design.

Several of the following settings were part of a "Spring Fever" show at Tiffany's, featuring a group of antique bird cages from Cooper Union as the centerpieces.

## The Golden Gridle and Pink Roses

Birds, butterflies, and flowers in spring's gay pastels form the central theme of this informal dinner table.

Guarded by a pair of sterling candlesticks, a Golden Gridle gazes out of his nineteenth-century inlaid wood and wire cage. Pink sweetheart roses decorate the feed boxes, and a butterfly hovers over the cage. A china pattern with pink roses and a pale blue border repeats the flower theme, as do the place mats, which are hand-blocked with pink and white flowers and green leaves. Horizontally feather-cut goblets and an English reproduction sterling pattern complete the setting.

This setting is bathed in soft grape and white colors, a harmonious and unusual color scheme. A grape-colored earthenware pattern is used with a combination of undecorated and ornate crystal—the cigarette urns and ashtrays have a contemporary look in contrast to the elaborately etched goblets. Guarding the covered tureen is the focal point of the setting, a pair of French porcelain birds on white perches, whose colors pick up the china pattern.

The cloth is all-important here. It was cut from a piece of pale grape and white figured cotton, chosen especially and only to complement this earthenware pattern. The decorative motif in the flatware design seems to repeat the figures in the cloth, as does the border design of the plates.

# A Grape-Colored Setting

A fresh, summery setting for a luncheon for four has been designed by Tate & Hall. Against a four-fold Chinese wood screen a round table is set, with an esthetic dedication to birds. A lemon-yellow cloth embroidered in varicolored feathers is a bright backdrop for the white dessert plates, each with a different hand-painted bird in the center. Ceramic clusters of grapes with removable tops hold cigarettes. The center accent of the table is a large basket of vermeil bamboo, filled with bright-colored fruit and green leaves. Vermeil leaf ashtrays and two crystal wine decanters shaped like saucy ducks add further accent. Especially unusual are the water goblets with their designs of etched birds—again, each one different; the wine goblets are of a simple, undecorated pattern. White and gold porcelain-handled flatware is the decorators' choice to complete the colorful table.

Hanging from the screen is a tôle bird cage, shaped like a palace, filled with tropical birds. The chairs provide a focal point; the *trompe l'oeil* designs are actually gay tôle replicas of wooden baskets filled with fruit.

# Birds and Fruit

DIANE TATE AND MARIAN HALL, INC. *Tiffany Decorators' Show*

# A Lilac Table

The lilac, one of spring's loveliest flowers, can freshen the table in any season with the advent of lifelike artificial flowers. In this luncheon setting a butterfly perches atop an antique bird cage in the center. The perky porcelain bird inside seems very much alive—indeed, he seems to sniff the pale lilacs in two crystal bud vases. The tablecloth is of mauve batiste in a lilac design; the white cotton napkins also feature a lilac print. The china pattern with tiny gold flowers on white is combined with slender, undecorated sterling water goblets and shell cigarette holders and ashtrays. The flatware honors the occupant of the cage—each size handle features a different bird in relief.

# The Black and White Table

A very definitely black and white table features a centerpiece of individual white porcelain roses and leaves, arranged in a white bisque urn. The white Boehm birds on either side of the porcelain flowers are used here as minor accents of decoration. A strong feeling of pattern is felt in the table. The gold-rimmed plates with black flowers on a white body repeat the feeling of the black print on the circular white cotton cloth. The black basalt coffee set and demitasse cups receive rich contrast from the gold of the vermeil tray, spoons, sugar tongs, and other accessories. Swedish crystal candlesticks and the simplest of champagne and water goblets add yet another note of crispness to this setting.

# A Conservative Luncheon Table

A mimosa-inspired setting for luncheon, with decorations of soft blue-green birds, a bird design on the china, and blue-green linen place mats. The yellow touches in the hand-painted birds on the plates are repeated in the porcelain bird figurine, and even more strongly in the bowl of flowers. The flatware, with its sculptured motif of birds in flight on the handles, is the perfect choice for a bird-lover.

# LUXURY
# TABLES

For four weeks Tiffany had the pleasure, courtesy of President and Mrs. Eisenhower, of showing to the public the late Margaret Thompson Biddle's collection of antique vermeil (sterling silver-gilt), which had been willed to the White House. Everything from punch sets to cigarette boxes, from knight figurines to wine coolers, was included in the White House collection. Shown here is part of a large formal dinner table, set entirely in vermeil with the exception of the crystal goblets, which was part of the exhibition. The center footed tureen is a very famous seventeenth-century piece of silver: it was the gift of Louis XV to the Prussian Ambassador to the Royal Court. The artichoke finial lends an attractive accent to this hand-some piece. To the left of it is one of a pair of covered tureens made by the English silversmith Paul Storr in 1806. The three-light candelabra are Sheffield (1821); the service plates, shell salt dishes, and flatware are also English, of a later period.

## The White
## House Vermeil
## Collection

# A Small Embassy Dinner

CLARE BOOTHE LUCE *Tiffany Hostesses' Show*

Clare Boothe Luce designed this dinner table along the lines of her small private parties at the Villa Taverna in Rome, when she was Ambassador to Italy. Her own antique English Georgian covered tureen in silver is used as the centerpiece, flanked by a pair of feather-cut candlesticks. Small, low bowls of striped carnations down the center are the only flowers. She uses elaborate blue, gold, and white china on the most delicate of lace mats made especially for her by Venetian lacemakers during her Ambassadorship. (She often uses these transparent mats over jewel-colored satin liners). The crystal goblets, in a thistle pattern, are of an unusual shape. She uses an ornate flatware pattern to coordinate with the other elements.

# The Turn of the Century

MRS. WILLIAM RANDOLPH HEARST  *Tiffany Hostesses' Show*

Mrs. William Randolph Hearst has set a table to recall with nostalgia another era—the turn of the century. In the "Mauve Era" the most elaborate of centerpieces would dominate the dinner party (Mrs. Hearst's is a monumental arrangement of fruit, vegetables, lilies, gardenias, and orchids). On a green satin cloth she has used richly-decorated service plates Tiffany made for her many years ago, as well as a sterling flatware pattern accented with inlaid copper called "The Aztec," designed exclusively for her by Tiffany's in the early twentieth century. Each handle has a different Indian motif sculptured on it. The excitement of the "Far West" permeated American design in this epoch.

In the closeup we see the detail on the interesting flatware, as well as the rococo candlesticks and Charles II covered cups flanking the centerpiece. The stemware is all Tiffany glass—the translucent iridescent "favrile glass" invented by Louis Comfort Tiffany. It became one of the leading elements of the "art nouveau" movement.

This whole table represents imaginative design and elegance from another era, a period of rapid growth in America's history, as well as in her economic power and cultural sophistication.

# Vermeil Dinner for Six

JANSEN INC. *Tiffany Decorators' Show*

Jansen of Paris and New York has designed a formal dinner in various shades of gold, with powder blue and white as blending colors. The antique chairs are of the Louis XVI period—white frames with incised velvet fabric—in a French powder blue.

Delicate white organdy linens with touches of gold embroidered flowers are used. Unembellished service and butter plates, shell-decorated flatware, and peppers and salts shaped like fish are all in vermeil. Heavy-cut crystal tumblers and white wine-filled decanters are the only crystal components on the table. Even the golden color of the wine is an important decorative accent. The centerpiece consists of an antique Chinese celadon dish filled with white carnations and yellow roses on a Louis XVI bronze doré base with sculptured figures blowing trumpets as the major motif. Flanking it are a pair of Directoire bronze doré candlesticks—again in a different shade of gold—with winged Pegasus figures.

The setting is placed against a four-panel screen of antique carved gilt wood frames encasing the blue and white silk damask fabric featuring classical Directoire designs.

# Midnight Supper for a Star

MELANIE KAHANE
*Tiffany Decorators' Show*

Melanie Kahane constructed an Edwardian pavilion for her "Midnight Supper for a Star," utilizing a color scheme she helped make famous—pink and orange. The two oyster-white brocade love seats with orange pillows are drawn up to a circular table covered with an embroidered pink cloth. Eighteenth-century English and German reproduction porcelain patterns in green, pink, orange, and white are used with vermeil flatware and holloware, including the energetic monkeys in court jester costumes which serve as candlesticks. An effective trick: the vermeil wine cooler holds a bottle of champagne surrounded by myriads of orange, pink, and white flowers tucked into the ice.

The top of Miss Kahane's pavilion is made of loosely shirred pink marquisette, while the carpet is of orange felt. The "star" and invited guest to this supper even has a jeweled bracelet wrapped as a gift at her place.

Mrs. Sheldon Whitehouse shows here her love of flowers in a dinner setting of sparkling white as a background for roses in shades of pink and red. She covers the table with her heavily embroidered white damask linens; the napkins are embroidered with the family crest. A simple antique silver basket fills the center of the table, inside a square of four of her gadroon-edge sterling candlesticks. On either side, her tall silver and mirrored plateaux hold full bouquets of roses ranging from palest pink to deepest red. Pink roses on the gold-bordered plates repeat the central theme.

Mrs. Whitehouse uses an elaborate tall-stemmed goblet pattern, but balances with it simple patterns of sterling flatware and small accessories for the table.

MRS. SHELDON
WHITEHOUSE
*Tiffany Hostesses' Show*

# A Dinner with Roses

# Dîner à la Russe

MRS. WILLIAM RANDOLPH HEARST, JR. *Tiffany Hostesses' Show*

Mrs. William Randolph Hearst, Jr., has set a dinner table with a Russian flavor of the nineteenth century. Flanking a crystal center-piece bowl of rose-colored carnations is a pair of rare six-light ormolu and rock-crystal candelabra, early nineteenth-century Russian, in the shape of tulips. Her china and linens belonged to her husband's grandmother, Mrs. Phoebe Hearst. The service plates are also early nineteenth-century Russian, featuring a strong green border design of animals of the hunt, and each plate containing a center armorial crest of the famous cities of Russia. Mrs. Hearst combines heavy crystal goblets of an ornate gold grape-leaf design with a shell-motif vermeil flatware pattern. All of the table accessories are in vermeil, from the covered boxes, eggs, and shell cigarette holders to the sculptured-rose menu holders. The rose motif is repeated again in the white damask cloth and napkins, luxuriously embroidered in wild roses on vines.

# Supper for Two on a Gueridon Table

SARAH HUNTER KELLY *Tiffany Decorators' Show*

Mrs. Sarah Hunter Kelly has done her supper for two in Chinese colors—black, gold and red. On an antique black and gold Bessarabian rug she has set a black lacquered round "Gueridon" table with gilt bronze feet in the shape of sphinxes. The design on the top of the table is in lovely soft reds and golds. The two chairs are Louis XV gilded bergères, covered in gray-green silk. The gilt bronze centerpiece holds delicate multicolored antique Saxe porcelain flowers and black candles. The service plates and flatware are of vermeil. Elaborately cut crystal goblets and écru linen and organdy napkins complete her table.

This kind of setting is designed to set off the beauty of the antique furniture and centerpiece. Elaborate linens or patterned porcelain objects would detract from the subtle harmony Mrs. Kelly has achieved in this design.

# The Small Table

# with Many Centerpieces

MRS. WILLIAM I. NICHOLS *Tiffany Hostesses' Show*

Mrs. William I. Nichols sets a dinner for two on a round table. She has successfully combined a mixture of colors, "looks," and periods in this small table that does not look at all cluttered. An enthusiastic "element" user, she combines a full range of crystal with a fruit centerpiece, a flower centerpiece, a girandole centerpiece, and even a bird centerpiece; wine decanter, footed compote for mints, salt and pepper, ashtrays, cigarette urns, and matches. The result is intimate and personal.

The circular cloth embroidered in green leaves and berries provides the backdrop. The formal plates have deep red and gold rims; the red is picked up in the cherries on the two-tiered fruit stand. The traditional goblet pattern coordinates with the decanter and the sparkling crystal girandole with three candles that provide the only illumination in the dining room. A Dorothy Doughty bird and flower figurine stands behind the bouquet of fresh pink posies.

# An Opulent Setting

WILLIAM PAHLMANN ASSOCIATES INC.

*Tiffany Decorators' Show*

Two ten-foot-tall Gothic screens form an impressive backdrop for William Pahlmann's dinner table. The screens immediately set the scene; made of ruby-red cut velvet on carved wooden bases, their reverse sides have borders embroidered with cardinals' hats in petit-point. Set on a flowered Aubusson rug, the unusual table is early nineteenth-century French with an oriental flavor in its strong design of mother-of-pearl marquetry. The chairs are English Regency, with seats covered in a striking red-striped silk. Mr. Pahlmann uses place mats and napkins of white linen with organdy insets. In the center is an antique white porcelain camel, carrying flowers in his pack and surrounded by clusters of red carnations and deep purple violets.

An oriental theme is advanced by using dinner plates with pastel chinoiserie figures ringing the gold border, combined with vermeil flatware and a cameo-decorated stemware. All of the table accessories are in vermeil. Behind the table is a rosewood coromandel cabinet holding a covered tureen and stand in red, gold, and white, flanked by vermeil compotes filled with mints.

# ACKNOWLEDGMENTS

The editors wish gratefully to acknowledge the cooperation of the following persons and organizations in the preparation of these table settings:

PHOTOGRAPHERS RESPONSIBLE FOR THESE PICTURES

Mr. Lee Prescott, Tiffany & Co.
Mr. Lee Cook, Tiffany & Co.
Mr. William Syzdek
Mr. Kal Weyner

ACCESSORIES

Abercrombie & Fitch Co.
Jack Borgenicht
City Knickerbocker, Inc.
George J. Coker & Son, Inc.
Gilford Leather Co., Inc.
Charles R. Gracie & Sons, Inc.
George Hartman
Susumu Ickta
John Mann

McArthur Shop Shells
Buddy Radisch
Schliemann-Borgos
Schrafft's
F. A. O. Schwarz
Silvestri Art Manufacturing Co.
David Weiss Importers
The Window Shop
Charles J. Winston & Co., Inc.

ANTIQUE FURNITURE AND ACCESSORIES

Accessories & Design, Inc.
Altman-Dwork, Inc.
The Antique Porcelain Co., Inc.
Ashley-Kent, Ltd.
Vladimir Barjansky
David Barrett
Jay Baumgarten Antiques
Sydney Brown, Inc.
The Collector's Corner
Country Imports, Inc.

Dalva Brothers, Inc.
French & Co.
H. Harmon Co., Inc.
Josephine Howell, Inc.
Jarvis Carriage House, Inc.
J. J. Klejman
Knoedler Art Galleries
Lavezzo, Inc.
Joseph Lombardo, Inc.
Needham's Antiques, Inc.

Nesle, Inc.
R. Olivieri
Frank Partridge, Inc.
Charles C. Paterson
Roslyn Rosier
Israel Sack, Inc.

Stair & Co., Inc.
Symons Galleries, Inc.
Transorient, Inc.
Frederick P. Victoria
J. J. Wolff Antiques, Ltd.

## CONTEMPORARY FURNITURE

Knoll Associates, Inc.
Laverne Originals
Mayhew

Paul McCobb Design Associates
Sandfort, Inc.

## FLOWERS AND GREENERY

Christatos & Koster, Inc.
Helen Cole, Inc.
Corteau Creations
Fellan Co., Inc.
The Gazebo

H. Carl Holpp & Co., Inc.
Judith Garden, Inc.
Max Schling, Inc.
Victoria Tree Florist
Wadley & Smythe

## LINEN, FABRICS, AND WALLPAPER

Emilia Bellini, Inc.
Louis W. Bowen
Brunschwig & Fils, Inc.
Thomas De Angelis, Inc.
Gladstone Fabrics
Hein & Kopins, Inc.
Leron, Inc.
Mosse, Inc.

Margaret Owens
D. Porthault, Inc.
Scalamandré Silks, Inc.
F. Schumacher & Co.
Siamese Imports Co.
D. D. & Leslie Tillett
George Tregard Co.
Woodson Wallpapers, Inc.

## RUGS AND FLOOR COVERINGS

Amtico
Ohan Berberyan
Archie Chamalian
Coury Rugs, Inc.
William J. Erbe Co.

Edward Fields, Inc.
Luten-Clarey-Stern
Silvestri
Stark Carpet Corp.
Ernest Treganowan, Inc.